The
GIANT
COMPASS

NAVIGATING YOUR LIFE WITH YOUR DREAMS

TERESA L. DECICCO, PhD

ISBN: 0-9812441-0-6

ISBN-13: 9780981244105

Library of Congress Control Number: 2008912111

MalitoPress

Printed in The United States of America

www.teresadecicco.com

Testimonials from People Who Have Used the Methods in this Book

I absolutely love these interpretation methods. Very easy to understand and to use.

This book is very useful because it teaches you dream interpretation but also how to understand the dreams in terms of waking life.

I was amazed at the revelations I had about my own life. Wonderful!

This has been one of the most interesting self-help books I have read. It does an excellent job of providing useful information that is extremely practical.

Dr. DeCicco is very knowledgeable in this area. She nicely explains the information for laypeople.

Great hands-on experience from this dream work!

This is some of the best material I have ever used. It's exciting and useful.

I love the methods in this book. It was so interesting to learn dream interpretation methods and then apply them with my own dreams. My dreams are now very beneficial to my waking life decisions.

The dream interpretation techniques in this book were incredibly effective.

The results from these interpretations can be remarkable.

Finally, science and self-guided dream therapy in one book. Very useful for my workshop participants!

This book has been most helpful for adding dream therapy into my professional practice. This provides tools for me to teach people how to help themselves.

Dedication

To the people who always believe in my dreams,
no matter what:

My strong and noble mother, Vincenza,

Matthew, who embodies pure energy and inspiration,

Anthony, who is endlessly wise and supportive,

My husband Walt for unconditional acceptance and
living the dream with me.

CONTENTS

CHAPTER THREE

CHAPTER FOUR

CHAPTER FIVE

CHAPTER SIX

CHAPTER SEVEN

CHAPTER TWELVE

CHAPTER THIRTEEN

A Note about the Dreams in This Book

All of the dreams in this book are from people who have volunteered their dreams for dream interpretation workshops or for research. Each dream was interpreted by the dreamer with one or more of the scientifically tested methods illustrated in this book. All the dreamers have remained anonymous, and complete confidentiality has been assured. Thank you to all the dreamers who shared their dreams and, consequently, helped shape this book.

CHAPTER 1

WHAT ARE DREAMS?
WHERE DO THEY COME FROM?

When the Mind Sleeps

A woman has a recurring dream that she is frantically running on the roof of a very tall building. Her feet are slipping from under her, her heart is pounding, and she is filled with fear. She feels a stranger chasing her, and though she can feel his presence, she has no sense of who he is. Suddenly, she stumbles and falls off the building. As she is free-falling through the air, she is thrashing and spinning and screaming for help, but no one can hear her. She wakes up in a sweat with a racing heart. The dream recurs in a similar way at least once per week and has done so for many years.

The human mind is a vast and boundless entity that is constantly active during the waking day, and then during sleep, it continues to assimilate and consolidate the stored information even more. Scientific studies have shown that during sleep time, the mind does not become dormant and inactive, but rather, it becomes busy and more productive than ever. Though most people don't realize it, their minds are just as active during some periods of sleep as they are in waking day. When the mind enters this essential and active state of sleep, then a fascinating and mysterious event is activated—the dreaming mind.

During dreaming, events of the past, present, and future come to life and play out in the nighttime images. It is here that the true "inner self" of the dreamer is revealed in many ways. The images are personalized with all the dream images and elements being created from the life of the dreamer. One of the most important elements generating and creating the dream imagery is the personality of the dreamer, which may be *the* most important aspect of dreaming.

Research has shown that it is, in fact, the personality of the dreamer that shapes and forms each image while generating the dream stories. For example, a person who is generally disagreeable with people in waking day will have more negative social interactions in dream imagery than a person who is generally agreeable. The dream images of a disagreeable person will have more people fighting or yelling than the dream images of an agreeable person. People who act out their aggression in a passive way in waking day will also have dream imagery that reflects this personality trait. Imagery can include such things as the dreamer's hair suddenly turning bright red in the dream, a group of strangers harming someone behind his or her back, or people sneaking and hiding while appearing to doing something devious. Similarly, people who are shy and quiet will find they don't have many people in their dreams while people who are extroverted and gregarious will have many dream characters.

The personality of the dreamer is clearly revealed in dreams through the images that are being created because the personality of the dreamer actually shapes and forms the dream images. Therefore, dreams are very important because they will reveal the true self of the dreamer, even if the dreamer is unaware of this. We are all somewhat blind to our own true personality, which, at times, can cause many problems in waking life. Unacknowledged anger can cause numerous relationship problems among family, friends, and co-workers. Extreme and unknown fears can block major opportunities in life. Stubbornness, often a real blind spot for people, can be the root of many negative life experiences for dreamers in waking life.

Similarly, positive personality traits can be unknown to the dreamer, but upon realizing them, this can lead the dreamer to many wonderful life events. The revelation of one's own altruistic personality can lead a dreamer away from an unfulfilling job to a fulfilling career in the helping profession. Realizing one's own high level of conscientiousness and great ability to deal with people may lead to a career in management. Similarly, realizing one's need for learning new things and having new experiences can lead to a decision of travel. No matter what the outcome of one's own personality, this knowledge can only help the dreamer find the perfect career, the right life partner, and the right life circumstances that will lead to joy.

Along with the personality of the dreamer, waking day experiences of the dreamer are also expressed clearly in the imagery of dreams. When looking closely at dream imagery, we can see that it reflects waking day behavior in many complex ways such that students in university dream about related events while people who are ill and visiting the doctor regularly have more medical imagery and related events in their dreams. People in committed relationships have different imagery than people in noncommitted relationships, and people who play sports dream about this more than people who do not play sports in their leisure time. It appears that dreams are a mirror image of one's waking life, but again, they will always be created in the paradigm of the dreamer's own personality.

Dream imagery gets even more personal and complicated since scientific studies have established that the dreamer's emotions are a major factor driving the imagery. The emotional life of the dreamer is clearly involved in the dream process such that people with a depressed mood will have more gloomy and dark imagery and also tend to have more negative outcomes. An anxious person will create imagery filled with anxiety, so typical anxiety dreams such as being chased or yelling but no voice being heard will be generated when the dreamer is highly anxious. Emotions in dreams are important information for the dreamer, especially if the emotions are unconscious to the dreamer in waking day. Most people will ignore emotions they are not comfortable with (e.g., I don't feel happy in this marriage anymore, I feel sad because I think my best friend is lying to me, or I'm unhappy in my job but I don't have the courage to change it) or simply repress them so they are not aware of their own emotional lives at all.

Dreams reveal emotions, which are one of the most important elements of the "true self" and are key elements in creating one's waking life circumstances. All decisions such as the choice to move to another city, leave a relationship, change career paths, have a baby, or simply spend more time with one's family are all emotionally driven. Not accessing the underlying emotions to decisions means that life is lived unconsciously and thus the choices being made may not be leading the dreamer to the best possible outcome. Fear may lead someone to stay in a town where jobs are scarce, unacknowledged anger may lead to isolation as all family and friends withdraw completely, and stubbornness may lead to a second or third divorce. Understanding one's own emotions means a more conscious life is being lived, and ultimately, decisions being made are based on one's highest life path—that is, decisions based on joy, happiness, and love rather than fear, worry, or anger.

Dreams get even richer with information since the desires, longings, and wishes of the dreamer's waking life are entwined with the dreamer's emotions. That is, those things that are deeply rooted in the consciousness of the dreamer but do not reveal themselves openly will appear in the dreaming mind. The desires, longings, and wishes, both at the conscious and unconscious levels, will clearly reveal themselves while the dreamer is in the sleep and dream state. It is here that the mind is processing and assimilating vast amounts of information, and thus, complicated information about one's true inner desires can be allowed to manifest without conscious control. The longing can be for any hidden desires: the need for a more loving or exciting marriage, the desire to have children while being married to a sterile spouse, the desire to travel the world, or to experience a new and exciting job. All of these longings will create images that directly reflect the "true self," the inner self that lies at the core of every individual and represents all complex levels of being. The dream images are not only a "fingerprint" of the dreamer, but also a complex map of the past, present, and future of the dreamer's whole life. There is a rich source of information being generated in dreams, and since the information is all about the dreamer and created by the dreamer, the information is never wrong.

So what does it mean when someone is being chased and then falling off a building during a dream? Both falling and chasing dreams are common dreams and always represent the dreamer's life and emotions. So if a woman has a recurring dream that she is being chased, falling off a tall building in a frantic state, and screams for help but no one can hear her, this represents events in her waking life and the emotions surrounding those events. If she felt exhilarated and excited in waking day, then the falling dream would be one filled with excitement and thrills; however, the frantic state she experiences in her dream state clearly reveals anxiety and possible fear in her waking day. This dreamer can work with the dreams to reveal those waking day situations that can be changed in order to relieve the anxiety and the fearful emotions that are being generated. Once the waking day situations triggering fear and anxiety are acknowledged and changed, then the dreams will stop.

When Dreaming Occurs

A woman dreams that she has cancer one week before the diagnosis from her doctor. She dreams that she has a large lump on her breast, and then her young son walks up to her and calmly says, "I see you have cancer, Mom."

The scientific community of consciousness has well researched and explored the realm of dreams and dreaming. Unfortunately, this information is rarely passed onto the non-scientific community in comprehensible ways. For example, it is now known that dreams are images and stories that are created "by" the dreamer from the dreamer's own deepest, unconstrained, innovative sleeping mind. Consciousness is creating and cocreating the imagery that reflects the dreamer's own life and future. Dreams are not random events but, rather, are direct images of a person's life and, most importantly, the dreamer's inner life and true self.

Scientific studies have shown that the dreamer creates these fascinating stories and images during deep sleep or REM (rapid eye movement) sleep. Though the dreamer rarely has control over these images, the images can unfold, shift, and weave incredible stories during each REM phase. Hence, night after night, REM period after REM period, dreams are being created and interweaved, whether the dreamer remembers them or not.

Since the beginning of time, people have been fascinated and curious about the dream images created in sleep because everyone dreams, whether they remember them regularly or just occasionally. Until scientific research was able to show that dreams relate specifically to the dreamer, people believed that dreams came from the outside world.

Along with this belief came the notion that dreams were from the occult, rooted in witchcraft or parapsychological phenomenon. Science today has shown us that the dreamer produces the dream images, and more importantly, they are incredibly relevant to many aspects of the dreamer's life. This makes dreams valuable sources of information from the dreamer about the dreamer. This information can then be used to help make decisions in one's life with respect to relationships, career, finances, or other major life events. Dream information can also be used as a guide in daily activities such as parenting, working, or socializing. They are proven to be a valuable and reliable gauge for living one's life fully, consciously, and purposefully.

How can a woman dream that she has cancer one week before her diagnosis? When the conscious mind is sleeping, the active dreaming mind can connect to all levels of being, especially the physical body. Through this mind-body connection, the mind can reveal in the dream state that the body has become ill thus bringing this information into the dreamer's awareness. The mind-body connection is one of the most important functions of the dreaming mind. It will alert the mind when the body is ill and will guide the dreamer to assessing the possibility of illness and then seeking out appropriate diagnosis and treatment.

The Dreaming Mind Knows More

For twelve years of marriage, a man has a recurring dream that he is being remarried. He sees himself at his own wedding and being married to a woman other than his current wife. He feels filled with joy and happiness while being married to a new person as all his family and friends are there to share in this celebration.

Dreams are produced during REM sleep when the brain is very active and able to produce flexible, creative, and playful images. The brain is able to pull images stored in memory that the conscious mind has long forgotten. The brain can also produce images that the conscious mind is not even aware of in waking day, such as unconscious beliefs, behaviors, emotions, and longings. All these images can then play together to arrange themselves and rearrange themselves to create any significant series of dream events. This is why dreams often have what appear as bizarre or confusing elements in them. For example, a house can appear as a house that was lived in as a child, but in the dream the house is also one's current home. This past/current home can also find itself floating nicely down a river as if it were a boat. When experiencing the dream, the dreamer knows exactly where he is and how it feels to be there. Upon waking, the dreamer may wonder how those images could possibly connect to waking life or make any sense at all. The dream images can be converted with dream interpretation from the dreaming mind into the waking mind, which then reveals important information about waking life.

Dream images are always telling the dreamer what he or she is actually creating in waking life. For example, if a woman says she wants to make her marriage work but constantly has dreams about being with another man, her inner self does not really want the marriage to work. Her thoughts and feelings, perhaps completely unconsciously, do not want to be in the current marriage, and her dreams will reveal those deepest feelings in her images.

Dreams reveal what the dreamer is thinking, feeling, and doing and, therefore, what he or she is manifesting in waking day. The images are a preview of how the dreamer is creating his or her life to be. If the dream reveals a life circumstance that the dreamer does not want, conscious awareness of the circumstance will help try and change it in waking life. Herein lies another important aspect of dreaming: the ability to see what one is creating in waking life, and then with that knowledge, being able to make changes in waking life and possibly change the outcome.

When a man dreams he is marrying someone other than his current spouse for twelve consecutive years, the dream is bringing up into his awareness deep feelings, deep longings, and perhaps a desire for something more than what his waking day relationship has offered. His desire for change may be with his current wife or it may not. Since the dreamer is in fact producing the dream, the dream is revealing his own inner self with all its complexities, and most importantly, the dream is never wrong. By becoming aware of the longings for a different kind of marriage, the dreamer can either begin changing his relationship with his current wife or look at leaving the marriage. He now has options to change his waking day situation and move toward a more positive outcome. He is not simply unconsciously participating in a marriage without knowing what is truly wrong and why he often feels empty and unfulfilled.

Making Dream Images

A woman dreams that she is in a hotel room with a co-worker and they have just had a passionate sexual encounter. In her dream, she feels sexually aroused and satisfied but is also filled with guilt and shame as she knows this is wrong since they *are both married. In the dream, she sits on the edge of the bed observing these feelings, and then her co-worker moves close to her and they begin having sex again.*

So what are these stories and scenes that are being created in dreams? The mind has stored every memory, every emotion, and every experience ever had. That is, every single memory including every book ever read, every person ever met, every television show watched, every emotion ever felt, and so much more. These memories, though long stored away from the conscious mind, can be accessed during sleep. Hence, dreams can produce images that may appear bizarre because they can include so many different elements from one's life. Many of those elements are so long forgotten that they appear foreign. A dream image of a childhood friend acting out in a current television program, which is occurring at the dreamer's workplace with all his neighbors and friends, can appear quite bizarre upon waking. In reality, all the images actually belong to the dreamer and represent different aspects of the dreamer's life. Though they may appear to be disjointed or bizarre in many ways, each element relates to the dreamer's life in some way.

Though the dreams connect to waking life, they also pertain to a deeper level of consciousness. The images will reveal the life that the dreamer is creating both consciously and unconsciously. They will reveal the people and events that the dreamer is attracting through thoughts and feelings. At this level, the dreams reveal the true inner self of the dreamer and ultimately the waking life that is unfolding.

Though the unconscious, sleeping mind of the dreamer produces the images, the conscious mind cannot often comprehend or connect them, given they are complicated and representative of so many different levels of the self. All that needs to be done is to recode the dream images into the dreamer's waking day understanding, and suddenly the disjointed, bizarre images become very meaningful. Not only are they meaningful, they can literally lead to waking day revelations that can transform one's life.

Research has shown that dreams with sexual content are more often about waking day relationships than they are about sex. In fact, relationship-related sex dreams have very different imagery than do dreams with sexual imagery that are, in fact, about sex alone. When a woman dreams that she is having sex with a co-worker and feels this is wrong, then dream interpretation on that imagery and the emotions around it will likely lead to waking day revelations about her marriage. This important information can then be carried into her waking life, which will give her insights on how to make her marriage better or indicate changes that she herself needs to make.

If Dreams Are So Important, Why Don't People Pay Attention to Them?

A man dreams that he is driving his car and begins to feel ill. He pulls over to the side of the road and suddenly begins to vomit. He notices that he is vomiting bright red blood. He feels very nauseous and dizzy to the point that the nausea wakes him up. He wakes up in his bed with the room spinning.

If dreams really contain important information about the dreamer and waking life, then why don't more people pay attention to their dreams? Many people do. Many people all over the world pay attention to their dreams and know that they are extremely important. In many cultures around the world, it is well known that dreams are part of consciousness and that paying attention to them will provide important insights about life. Cultures from the beginning of time have said that dreams are important, but unfortunately, over time, dreams have been ignored or marginalized in some parts of the world.

The main reason for this is that when the Bible was translated by St. Jerome in the fourth century, he changed the meaning of "dreams" to be associated with "witchcraft" throughout the Bible. As a result, this caused people in the Christian world to stop looking at their dreams. This aspect of the inner self and the cocreation of that self with the world has become unknown to many people. The greatest loss is that the important and direct information between one's life path and one's dreams is interpreted to be unconnected. What many people don't understand is that their life path and their dreams are *completely connected*—matters such as: Who should I marry? How can I find my soul mate? What job will bring me more money? How can I make more money and be happy? How can I lose weight? How can I improve my health? What will happen to me when I die? As decisions are made about these life-altering issues, then one's dreams will not only reflect that, but they will act as a guide in the decision making process. If the dreamer is choosing a wrong life partner, the dreams will signal that. If someone is holding on to an unfulfilling job, the dreams will signal that. If behaviors are starting to cause illness in the body, the dreams will signal that as well. Dreams can be used as clues to deciphering one's ultimate life path and can provide direction and opportunities to live a more fulfilling, healthy, and joyous life.

This book is for those people who want to begin tapping into their own deepest wisdom to help them with their life questions. People who pay attention to their lives, watch for clues from their dreams, and then make adjustments in waking life based on the information in dreams can follow the highest path in the direction that their lives are ultimately meant to go. The deepest part of the self is speaking in dreams, and by becoming aware of this information, the mystery of one's life slowly unravels. By deciphering the meanings in dreams, one can be led to the best job, the ultimate partner, the unending source of money, the best decisions about health, and the answers to life after death.

The first step in getting a clearer understanding of one's own life through dreams is to begin working with them— that is, to begin a practice of dream interpretation that works. Dream interpretation techniques should be scientifically tested, as are other forms of therapy, to ensure that they, in fact, lead the dreamer to valid insights. Since dreams are part of the psyche, one should not tamper or play with them, but be respectful and cautious as you would with any other form of treatment or intervention. Therefore, only scientifically tested methods will be used in this book. The methods all provide privacy. They are proven to lead to waking day insights and have been tested scientifically against control groups.

Once the practice of dream interpretation is underway and insights are gained, the next step is to take the information from the dream and begin incorporating that into waking life. The process is such that more dreams will continue to guide the dreamer based on the steps taken in waking day. Once decisions are made and action is taken in waking life, then dreams act as a guide on that path of action. Generally, dreams and dream interpretation act as a life long, on-going guide to one's life and life's constant changing challenges.

So if a man dreams he is vomiting blood, the first step in waking life is to look at his waking day behavior. If he does not live a healthy lifestyle or engages in health-compromising behavior such as smoking, drinking alcohol, or over-eating, the dream may be making him aware of the health risk. If going to the doctor is appropriate, the doctor may recommend treatment because he is in fact at risk of heart disease. Should he ignore the doctor's advice, another health-warning dream is likely (dreams tend to recur when waking day situations have not changed!). If he changes his diet, takes blood pressure medication, and quits smoking, his dreams may reveal that he is getting healthier.

Why Are Dream Messages Not More Obvious?

A woman dreams she is going out on a date with a man she has just met. She is all dressed and ready to go out on her date when he shows up. Just as they are getting into his car to go, she says she has forgotten something, so she runs into her garden shed. She then takes out a large machete and puts it into her purse.

If dream imagery is so important, why are the messages not more obvious? For many people they are. They are obvious to people who work with them every day. Dream interpretation often begins as a mysterious and complicated event, but slowly, while doing systematic dream interpretation, the meanings reveal themselves clearly. After practicing dream interpretation for some time, the meanings become second nature and more obvious. Once dream awareness is assimilated into one's life, the message is often clear upon waking. More importantly, the next logical step in waking life is apparent as well.

The process of deciphering one's dreams and ultimately one's life path does not usually happen instantly. This process evolves over time as dream interpretation is practiced. The practice becomes easier and more efficient but it is a practice. As with anything new in life, such as learning to ski, paint landscapes with watercolors, or bake pastry, it takes time, patience, and practice. As time goes on and dream interpretation is practiced, the messages become clear, and the mystery of one's life beautifully reveals itself. This is one of the most rewarding and exciting practices that someone can undertake—a journey toward a fulfilling life.

Science knows a great deal about dream generation and how each individual is creating images that are filled with rich, complex, intricate information about the dreamer and waking life circumstances. These images are a valuable source of information to the dreamer and the key to making them indispensable is to translate the dream images into productive information in the waking mind of the dreamer. The chapters that follow will begin the process of dream interpretation in a scientifically proven system. The methods that are taught are user friendly and straightforward and predict insight into the dreamer's life. Each interpretation builds on the previous one and takes the dreamer deeper and deeper into the meaning of dreams. The real jewel lies in the fact that dreams carry information about the past and the present that can then help create the dreamer's future yet to come.

A woman dreaming that she has put a machete in her purse before a date can expose her waking day dating life. Upon doing dream interpretation, she may find that she is really afraid of the man that she is dating and should stop seeing him. The interpretation may also reveal that she needs to protect herself emotionally since in past relationships, she has gone into relationships too quickly and with reckless abandon. No matter what the insight for her, the dream will guide her to a healthier relationship in waking day if she is aware of the message and willing to hear it.

The Dreamer as Expert

A sixteen-year-old boy who is suffering from a chronic and serious illness dreams that his family is discussing the possibility of putting him to death. He sees his old cat who has died six months previously sitting at his feet, and she is partially decayed. Some of the family members agree to sign the consent form for his death and others do not.

Contemporary writers and researchers now agree that the dreamer is the one who really knows the true meaning of the dream. Therapists, guides, or dream workshop leaders can lead dreamers to finding their dream's meaning, but they cannot tell the dreamer what a dream is actually about. The dream's imagery is so specific to the dreamer and to his or her life that the dreamer has to interpret the imagery. No one can do this for the dreamer, but techniques, such as the ones in this book, can lead the dreamer to his or her own insights.

Dream imagery is very specific to the dreamer and each dreamer's life, so only the dreamer will know what an image means for him or her. For example, if a woman is phobic of dogs and dreams about a dog, she may interpret this to mean something about fear and anxiety. If another woman loves dogs and has four of her own, she may interpret dream image of a dog to be about love and companionship. Another woman who is a dog breeder may find dream imagery of a dog to be about income. These examples clearly indicate the specificity of dream imagery for each dreamer and how only the dreamer will really know what each image means to him or her.

A note about dream dictionaries—dream dictionaries are fun to consult and interesting to read but should be used with caution in terms of interpreting one's dreams. Dream dictionaries often assume that one image means the same thing for all people. Though there may be some universal images, it is more often the case that dream imagery has been created by the dreamer in terms of the dreamer's unique personality and life circumstances. By working with one's own dream images and learning how to interpret them, a dreamer is unlocking the treasure box of insight, guidance, and transformation.

The young man who has had a dream about his decaying cat and his family contemplating his death can do dream interpretation to reveal issues around death, dying, and family. This type of rich and revealing dream can help him to cope with his chronic illness as well as with members of his family. Also, by actively facing fears around death through dream interpretation, this young man can become more peaceful in his daily life.

How Do We Know That Dreams Really Work?

A woman has a dream that she is on an elevator and gets off at the twenty-fifth floor of a building. When she gets off, she is at the symphony where an older man is waiting for her. He approaches her nervously and asks if she would be interested in going to dinner with him. When she accepts his invitation, he is very relieved and says: "I'm so happy you will have dinner with me—since I'm seventeen years older than you, I wasn't sure you would say yes."

The age-old question is often still asked: do dreams contain meaningful information, or are they just events caused by random brain activity and really have no meaning at all? Scientists who study the consciousness of dreams have discovered that dreams are meaningful and contain information reflecting the life path of the dreamer. However, this finding can and should be put to the test by anyone who would like to use his or her dreams in a meaningful way.

If dreams are relevant and meaningful to one's life, then anyone can watch their dreams, watch what is happening in their daily lives, and see if in fact the two are related. According to scientific findings, what is happening in waking day should be reflected in one's dreams. It may take some practice, but watching and noticing the events of one's daily life and one's dream life will reveal if the two are truly related.

More importantly, dream interpretation will reveal how the dream images are related to one's life. For example, if a man is caring for his elderly, ill mother, he may find that he is dreaming about her. Dream interpretation may reveal that he has a deep desire to forgive his mother for the many instances in life where she hurt him. The dreams may also reveal that he needs to do this before she dies in order to free himself of any life-long pain he has been carrying from his relationship with his mother. The dreamer should then ask the following questions: Does this actually relate to my life? Are the dream events a projection of my waking day events? Does the meaning derived from the dream interpretation reflect my true feelings?

Only by putting one's own dreams and dream interpretations to the test will answer the age-old question. How can one really know if dreams are meaningful to waking life and if they should be used as a compass to navigate one's life course? They should only be used if they reveal themselves to be true for the dreamer.

After having a dream about being at the symphony, this woman goes to the symphony with a friend in waking life. She is then introduced to an older man by her friend who later asks her out for dinner. Having had the dream, she accepts the invitation, and they begin a happy, loving, long-term relationship. She uses the emotions and signals from the dream as a guide to her decision of whether or not to see him in waking life.

CHAPTER 2

WHAT ARE YOUR DREAMS TELLING YOU?

Everything in Dreams

A man dreams he is at his cottage, and while he is out on his boat watching the beautiful sunset, he suddenly sees his place of employment appear in the distance. As he nears the shore, he sees the building he works in and his co-workers all talking and mingling outside the building.

While sleeping and dreaming, the brain wave patterns allow the mind to bring up images, play with them, and recreate many thoughts, feelings, and behaviors that the waking mind simply cannot do. So what are dreams telling the dreamer in those images? Absolutely everything that is important in the dreamer's life. Once the dreamer is aware of this, the information can then be assimilated into waking life, which can have a huge impact on future waking day events.

A man may dream that his is spending too much time working and playing golf and not spending enough time with his family. Upon dream interpretation, he comes to this realization because in waking day, he was completely oblivious of the impact of his actions on his family. He can then choose to balance his family life, work life, and leisure time, which will result in a completely new life for him and his family for years to come. Alternatively, he can continue doing what he is doing but armed with the knowledge that he may damage his family life permanently. Either way, the dream has brought the information to his awareness, and he is choosing his life path knowing this.

There is no doubt from scientific research and clinical findings that dreams have incredible transformative potential for the dreamer. These nighttime stories are communicating important information back to the dreamer about waking life. The information can range from health issues to relationships, finances, and major life decisions. The information is as vast and unique as the dreamer's own life.

A man who is dreaming about his workplace being at his cottage may find upon dream interpretation that he is carrying his work with him everywhere, and perhaps this is impacting negatively on his life. He may discover from dream interpretation that his work is no longer fulfilling to him and a change is needed. Whatever the insight, the most important finding is that the interpretations will be specific to him and his own unique life experiences; he can then choose waking day behaviors accordingly.

The Physical Body and Dreams

A woman dreams that she is looking at her co-worker, and suddenly the co-worker's dress falls off. She notices that the co-worker keeps working and doesn't notice her dress has fallen off but that she has a huge black and red bruise on her thigh. The co-worker continues to work without paying attention to her wound. The woman looks at the huge wound and immediately begins to feel sick to her stomach.

Some of the most important information conveyed in dreams is information about the dreamer's physical body. The body is represented in dream imagery, so information about health and safety can often be conveyed. Common dreams that are health related will alert the dreamer to health problems through the mind-body connection of dreaming.

The mind and the body are completely connected, so when something happens in the body, the mind is aware of it. That does not mean it is in conscious awareness because awareness can be in the unconscious mind. Therefore, the mind can know when the body is healthy and well, and it can also know when the body is becoming ill. If someone is ill but still unaware of the illness, the mind can know this and reveal the information in the form of dreams. The body may not yet experience pain or have any visible symptoms of the illness, but this does not mean that illness is not present. Health dreams are very useful because they tell the dreamer about what condition the body is in. This vital information can then be used to take the necessary steps toward proper health care in waking life. For example, early detection and treatment may result from awareness of health dreams.

Similar to illness or health dreams, dreams can bring health-compromising behavior into the awareness of the dreamer. If high-risk behavior such as smoking, excessive drinking, drug abuse, or any other illness-related behavior is occurring in waking day, then dreams can depict this. Dreams that portray health-compromising behavior may also depict the demise of the dreamer if the behavior is not changed. For example, a man dreamt that he was looking over his dead body with a glass of liqueur in one hand and a hash pipe in the other. In waking day, he was, in fact, using drugs and alcohol in a very unhealthy manner. This warning dream very clearly told him that continued drug and alcohol use would result in his death. In this instance, the warning dream could not be clearer. The body sent the mind information in the form of dream imagery to warn him of his demise.

Another important way that dreams are helpful is in the treatment for illness and disease. The body knows if the treatment is working and healing the illness and when it is not. Therefore, the effects of any form of treatment such as surgery, medication, or acupuncture may be revealed in dreams. If the treatment is working, the dreams will reveal positive, healthy, and healing imagery. This is also an indication that the treatment should be continued. If the treatment is not working, dreams may reveal negative health imagery or even warning dreams. This provides valuable insight into waking life, so the dreamer can reassess current treatment and its benefits and also may explore possible alternatives.

When a woman had a dream that her co-worker's dress fell off to reveal a huge black and red bruise on her leg, she discovered with dream interpretation that this is a health-warning dream. The dream may be about her own health or about the health of a close friend or relative. Dream interpretation will unravel the imagery to reveal information about the illness and what possible steps needed to be taken in waking day.

What We Think About, We Dream About

A young man dreams that he is at his grandmother's house and sitting at her kitchen table. His grandmother walks in with a tray of chocolates and offers him a chocolate. He takes a chocolate and then stands up and lovingly gives her a big hug.

Consciousness is continuous. The brain is busy and active in each moment of life, including sleep time. In waking day, the mind is constantly active with conscious thoughts and feelings: thoughts about relationships (e.g., why am I having such a bad time with my boyfriend?), thoughts about work (e.g., why is this co-worker so difficult to work with?), thoughts about everything and anything that the mind can hold onto. These thoughts and the feelings triggered from them are then carried into the sleep state from the waking state.

In the sleep state, these thoughts continue to process and assimilate information that has been generated in waking day. Therefore, these thoughts are brought into the dream state and generate dreams that incorporate waking day thoughts and feelings. The actual thoughts and feelings that the dreamer has all day long are embedded in the dreams.

When a woman is having trouble with her teenage daughter in waking day, she may think about her daughter's negative behavior often throughout the day. She thinks about how her daughter does not cooperate with the family. She thinks about how her daughter often stays out late with her friends, sleeps late into the day, and then spends most of her time getting ready to go out with her friends again. She plays over and over in her mind how her daughter is defiant when asked to participate in family events or to do simple things like clean her room or the kitchen after she has used it. The mother thinks about negative discussions she and her daughter have had in the day. She even ruminates about what she should do with her. Should she demand that she move out? Should she demand that she participate in the family? Should she go to counseling? And on and on her mind chatters about her problem. These thoughts are then carried into the night, and as she sleeps she continues to produce more thoughts and feelings around the issue. This woman will then dream about her daughter and the situation they are in. She will also dream about possible solutions since she has been thinking about that in waking day. She will create imagery that is charged with all the waking day emotions surrounding her daughter and the situation.

If the dreamer has thoughts of worry and rumination then that shows up in the imagery. The conscious thoughts about life and circumstances will all show up in dream imagery.

Therefore, the dreams tell the truth that lies within the dreamer's mind.

Of course people are not necessarily conscious of their thoughts in waking day, just because they are having them. Most people are quite unconscious to the thoughts that continue to rattle on within them. In fact, it is not until thoughts are in conscious awareness does a person even know they exist. Dream interpretation is one important way that a dreamer will realize what they are really thinking about in waking day.

An example of this phenomenon is illustrated in the following. Someone portrays himself as honest and ethical in a business deal. He believes himself to be honest and trustworthy. Unknown to himself and to the other partners in the deal, this person is often thinking, ruminating, and imagining ways to make the deal happen in an unethical manner. In his unconscious mind, he is willing to forgo his ethics so the deal will go through, no matter what. He is willing to do this because of the money he can receive from this deal. In therapy, he reveals that he dreamt about the deal going through but that he was wearing a black cloak and hood, and his partners did not know it was him. Upon dream interpretation, he discovers that he is more focused on making the deal happen in any way possible, even in an unethical manner, than honoring everyone involved in the deal. What he thought and felt all day long in his private, confidential thoughts continued to process while sleeping and dreaming. One cannot hide from his own true thoughts and feelings in dream images.

A young man who thinks and feels lovingly about his grand-mother will have dreams that reflect this. A dream that the young man is in his grandmother's kitchen where she is offering him chocolates illustrates how loving and generous the young man feels his grandmother is toward him. When they hug with love and affection, this image discloses the emotions they truly feel for each other. This dream is a clear continuation of waking day thoughts, feelings , and experiences for the young man.

What We Don't Think About, We Dream About

A wealthy, successful woman has a recurring dream that she has lost her wallet and all her money. She dreams that her wallet is missing from her purse, and then when she goes to the bank to get money, they tell her that she has no money in her accounts. She is afraid and anxious in the dreams and never finds her wallet or her money.

As discussed previously, people can have thoughts and feelings that they are unaware of. They can also have feelings without any thoughts attached to them and be completely unaware of those feelings. This is a level of feeling that is deeply unconscious—the deepest feelings, hopes, longings, and wishes that the person is not aware even exist. Not surprisingly, these too will find their way into the dreamer's imagery.

When these images appear, the dreamer often does not recognize them until dream interpretation reveals the true meaning at a conscious level. These feelings lie so deeply within the psyche that they can appear foreign to the dreamer.

What is the benefit of bringing these feelings into conscious awareness? Since waking lives are driven, created, and formed by thoughts and feelings, then being unaware of one's feelings means that one's life is being created unconsciously. When life is being created unconsciously, then events appear to happen without any control. If a man is unaware that he harbors deep, unconscious anger, then all of his relationships will be contaminated with anger, unknown to him. He may not know why his children have abandoned him, why his two marriages have failed, and why he is constantly having negative interactions at work. The world appears hostile and out to destroy him. Once he realizes that he is carrying deep-rooted anger into all his life experiences, he can see that this anger has created all the situations and relationships around him. Every experience and relationship is shrouded in his anger because this is what he is bringing into every situation. Conscious awareness of this deep emotion can lead to a major revelation. This revelation can then change waking day circumstances dramatically. This man can literally change his life by the realization of his own unconscious emotions and choosing to behave differently.

When a wealthy and successful woman dreams that she has lost her wallet and all her money, the dream is revealing her true and deepest feelings around money. Even though she is successful, her anxiety and fear around money is obvious. This fear may be causing her to be a workaholic or to work at a career that she deeply dislikes but does it only for the money. Any number of negative waking day situations could result from her deep-rooted fear. Awareness of this negative relationship with money can help her to work toward overcoming her fear and bettering her life.

Relating to Relationship Dreams

A woman dreams that she is having dinner at her daughter's home. She notices that there are many people around the table, but no one is speaking to her. She sees them talking amongst each other, but no one will speak to her. She gets angry as she gets up from the table to leave. She goes to the front closet and pulls out two pigs' heads. She puts one head under each arm and storms out of the house.

Perhaps one of the greatest sources of information from dreams is the image relating to the dreamer's interpersonal relationships. Waking day relationships are one of the greatest sources of pleasure and sources of challenge for people. Since relationships with parents, partners, children, friends, co-workers, and many others are so paramount in people's lives, issues revolving around relationships clearly show up in the dreamer's nighttime mentations. The importance of relationship dreams is that they can be examined for personal and social insights that will help dramatically in waking day.

Research has found, for example, that most dreams with sexual imagery are interpreted to be about waking day relationships and not to be about sexual relationships. Since dreams with sexual imagery are common and typical, they can be an important source of information about waking day relations. Interpreting dreams with sexual imagery can be a useful tool for getting insight into relationships, for revelations about relationships, and for tapping into the deepest and perhaps unconscious emotions that lie within relationships.

Upon interpretation of a dream with sexual imagery, a woman may find that she is neglecting her spouse or that she has stopped engaging in the relationship in a warm and loving manner. With this awareness, she can now begin making changes in her waking day relationship that can transform the relationship and, in turn, her life.

Dreams without sexual imagery can also be about many waking day relationships. Relationships with parents, children, friends, co-workers, or neighbors can all appear in dreams if they are important in waking day. Since relationships are so important in daily life, these also tend to be one of the most important forms of dream imagery. The interpretation of the imagery will reveal if the relationship is harmful, if love is being shared between people, or if the relationship is making someone sick due to toxic behaviors. All of this information and more will come up when the mind is in the sleep and dream state.

A woman dreams she is in her wedding dress and ready to be married. She suddenly finds herself in a jail cell, and she cannot get out. There is, in fact, no door to the cell. Upon interpretation, she finds that the current romantic relationship she is in demands that she keep herself in a box. That is, she cannot be fully herself but must keep parts of herself hidden and constricted. For example, her openness to travel and curiosity about other cultures is one aspect of her personality that she cannot allow to be expressed while she is in this particular romantic relationship. Upon discovering this in her conscious mind from dream interpretation, she can now make a decision about her waking life circumstances. She can choose to leave the relationship and fully be herself or stay and accept the fact that she has to change parts of herself in order for the relationship to survive. If she chooses the latter, she is doing so with complete conscious awareness, and she will not fight against the need to express herself. She will be in the relationship with acceptance and understanding of how things are. If she chooses to leave and be in another relationship, she will know that the relationship must allow her to fully be herself.

Dreams will also be helpful with family relationships. If parents and children are struggling to be harmonious, then dreams will reveal the source of the disharmony and may provide possible solutions to the problems. Often family struggles get people locked into power struggle or locked into patterns that cause more difficulty. Revelations about one's own behavior as well as the behavior of others will help in these waking day relations.

A woman who dreams of putting two pigs' heads under her arms finds in dream interpretation that she is "too pig headed." This astonishing discovery about herself causes her to look deeply into her own behaviors and how she has contributed to her disharmonious relationships. She can begin the process of self-realization, and if willing, she can now change her own behavior and change her family relations. While changing one's own behavior is not easy, the conscious awareness that the behavior exists is the crucial first step.

Nightmares

A young mother dreams that she sees her eighteen-month-old toddler playing at the beach with his father. They are at a distance so they cannot see or hear her, but she can see them. The father suddenly throws an apple into the water and turns his back on the baby. The baby begins to walk into the water after the apple. The mother knows he will drown if he falls down, and she is too far away to get to him. The father has no idea that his baby is wading farther and farther into the water. The mother watches her baby from a distance and finds herself in a frozen panic.

Nightmares are a special kind of anxiety dream. Some researchers have devoted their entire area of study to these alone, trying to uncover why they occur and also how to stop them. If someone is suffering from nightmares on a regular basis, then dream interpretation alone is not likely going to help them. Treatment of severe nightmares is beyond the scope of this book, and therefore, professional help should be sought from a medical doctor, psychologist, or therapist.

For occasional nightmares, dream interpretation can be very useful, especially if the nightmare is a recurring dream, but not as frequently as on a weekly or nightly basis. In these cases, as with all recurring dreams, there is a waking day circumstance that the dreamer is not attending to, and therefore, the consciousness of the dreamer is manifesting the information in the form of a nightmare. For example, a man works in a factory with large machinery and has a recurring dream that he accidentally gets caught in the machinery and gets ground up. It is likely that the dream is alerting him to his work situation. It may be that the environment is literally a dangerous one and poses physical danger to him. Alternatively, the work environment may be too stressful for him and contributing to his waking day unhappiness, which is literally grinding him down. Dream interpretation with occasional nightmares is extremely useful and can provide insight at many levels of waking life.

A young mother who is watching her son about to drown in a dream can interpret this dream with any number of techniques and find meaning. She may find that the father is not as attentive to his children as he should be in waking life, and therefore, she needs to accommodate this to ensure their safety. Alternatively, she may find that she is overly worried about her children's safety, and this may, in fact, be causing her unnecessary anxiety in waking day. Upon assessing the situation of waking day and comparing this to her dream insight, she can adjust her behavior accordingly. That is, she can be more watchful of her children if their father is not, or she can see that she is overly worried for no reason and decrease her waking day anxiety. Either way, the dream insights help her parent her children in a healthy way.

Death, Dying, and Beyond

A woman dreams that her deceased infant son, who died thirty years previous, comes to her and tells her to stop being so sad. She can feel and hear him in the dream, but she cannot see him. Upon waking she feels this short but vivid dream is very important but not sure how it relates to her current waking life.

Dreams about death, dying, and what lies beyond the physical body, are perhaps one of the most common and feared dreams of all. People often dream about death, their own or someone else's, and the biggest fear is that the dream will, in fact, come true. Research on death dreams and the dreams of the dying reveal many important findings about death imagery.

First, if someone is afraid of death, thinks about death in a negative way, or represses feelings around death, then this imagery will show up in dreams. Death imagery will reveal the waking day thoughts, feelings, and emotions of the dreamer. The most important waking day contribution this imagery can reveal is that the dreamer can begin working with the notion of death in waking life. The dreamer can face the existential issues of death, fear of death, and any spiritual beliefs of the afterlife that are being revealed in dreams.

These can be examined on a conscious level and then incorporated into the dreamer's waking life. The result of facing one's fear of death is that life is lived more fully. One does not waste a day or even a minute of waking life once the inevitability of death is faced. Living in denial of death may lead to unconscious apathy or squandering precious daily life. The reality of eventual death should lead to consciously fulfilling each and every day.

Dreams can also push one's true life purpose to the forefront of one's life, so that meaningless or dreaded activities are avoided. Waking life becomes purposeful, joyful, conscious, and deeply meaningful once death has been reconciled. Dreams can play a part in that reconciliation if the dreamer is willing to pay attention and work with the dreams.

A woman dreamt that she was with a co-worker who led her into a small airplane. The airplane flew like a helicopter and went straight up into the sky, far above the clouds. The plane kept going up higher and higher until she reached a very bright light. The door of the plane opened, and she saw her deceased aunt outside of the door. The aunt simply said to her that she was fine, she was happy, and no one should worry about her. Upon waking, the dreamer began reading and journaling about death. She tried to face her fear of death by educating herself about the issue. Her readings led to her to people she could talk to about death and to discovering her own spiritual beliefs. More dreams about spiritual matters then led to her to her own beliefs about life, its purpose, and her own death.

When a woman dreams about her deceased son, this can have several important meanings for her. The words "don't be so sad" may be a reminder about her own actions in current waking day. If she connects the dreams to her waking life, she may find a revelation about her own behavior. The dream imagery may also be reminding her that she still has to reconcile the fact that her infant son had passed away. Deep emotions on this issue will surely be affecting her waking life, so the dream may guide her to deal with these feelings. Death dreams are filled with important information for the dreamer about the dreamer's life and, more importantly, about spiritual and end of life issues.

The Purpose of This Book

A teacher dreams that she is away in a strange land and traveling with a group of people she does not recognize. She suddenly sees a sign that tells her she is in a rural town in India. The dream then shifts, and she is in a classroom in India and teaching small children who are all smiling back at her.

Since dreams are all about the dreamer's own life and they are never wrong, it is very important to first become aware of one's own dreams, to interpret them properly, and then to make appropriate adjustments in waking life based on the meaning of the dream. This is where dreams can have tremendous transformative potential and can literally help people change their lives. The purpose of this book is to first help dreamers become aware of their dreams by remembering and recording them. Once this awareness has occurred and dreams are remembered, then dream interpretation can begin. This book will provide four dream interpretation techniques that have been scientifically tested, are known to lead to insights about waking life and other life issues, and are easy to use. Each of the techniques build on each other until more and more information is extracted from the dreams.

The first technique is The Storytelling Method of Dream Interpretation. This method connects dream imagery directly to waking life situations of the dreamer. This technique has been scientifically tested and is known to link the imagery to the life of the dreamer in meaningful ways. The technique must be used with the worksheet provided in this book. If the worksheet is not used, the interpretation does not lead to meaningful insights. After using the technique with several dreams and getting comfortable with dream interpretation, the next method adds an important component to dream interpretation: extracting the *emotions* that drive the imagery.

The 2A-Method of dream interpretation has similar principles to The Storytelling Method, but this method works with the emotions surrounding and driving the images of a dream. This method is particularly useful to begin a deeper understanding of dream interpretation and to get to a deeper level of understanding of what consciously and unconsciously the dreamer is creating in waking day life.

A third method of interpretation, The Projective Method, will then be covered. This is a group-sharing method that has been shown to be useful for deriving the meaning from dreams with the assistance of other people. This method ensures that personal, private, and confidential material in dreams is not shared with others, but at the same time, useful interpretations may arise from sharing the dream in a systematic way. This method can be used with family members, dream workshop members, or any group of people who are interested in working with dreams together.

The last method is Meditative Dream Re-Entry (MDR). This method is used once dreamers are comfortable with working with their dreams and are able to derive meaning from their dreams at many different levels. That is, dreams are known to be about waking life, about deep emotions, and about life issues at many different levels. It may take weeks or even months before this level of comfort is reached, but once it is, then the dreamer can go even deeper into the meaning of dreams with MDR.

With the use of simple relaxation techniques, the dreamer is first to practice relaxation twice a day for two weeks. This allows the chatting, conscious mind to relax and begin processing at a different wavelength than when the mind is busy. After several weeks of practicing relaxation, then Dream Interpretation Imagery can be used. This visual imagery exercise guides the dreamer into a dream and allows the dream to unfold and continue such that a deeper meaning and deeper understanding of the imagery can be revealed. This level of dream interpretation will combine the emotional component with multiple levels of imagery at the same time. The result is a rich and meaningful transformation of the imagery into the waking consciousness of the dreamer. Since the dreamer is the best expert on his or her own life, dreams will reflect back all the important life information that needs to be given attention in waking day. Here lies the fundamental inner self that creates one's life as it is unfolding in each moment.

The teacher who dreams of teaching in India has a great revelation with dream interpretation that she would like to teach abroad. She is happy to discover in waking life that she can take a leave of absence for a year and travel to a foreign land to teach. Through her dream work, she has found her purpose, which is to share her gift of teaching and the love of learning with people around the world.

CHAPTER 3

TIPS FOR RECALLING DREAMS

Pay Attention

An eighty-year-old woman has been having the same dream theme for over six decades. She dreamt in high school that she was lost and could not find her classroom. When she arrived at the classroom, she was in the wrong room and didn't recognize the teacher. After high school, the dream imagery changed so she had a recurring dream that she could not find her house. When she finally arrived at her home, she had lost her keys. Upon realizing that she lost her keys, she would get very upset and began frantically looking for them.

We know from scientific research that everyone dreams including children, adults, and people from every culture around the world. Though not everyone remembers their dreams, dreaming occurs about every ninety minutes during sleep. When people are not remembering their dreams, just a few subtle changes can trigger the mind into remembering them upon waking. The key to getting useful information from dreams starts with training the mind to remember them.

Once the dreamer decides that dream information is important and valuable, the mind will then begin to focus on that. That means dreams will be remembered upon waking because the conscious mind has decided that they are now important. At first they may be short or vague. The dreams may just be a feeling with no visual or auditory imagery. In time, they will become much more vivid and detailed. Just as dream interpretation must become a practice, remembering to remember dreams must also become a practice. In time, as dream interpretation becomes second nature so will remembering dreams.

For six decades a woman has the recurring dream of being lost or losing something important. Recurring dreams are telling the conscious mind that there is something in waking day that needs to be changed or attended to. This woman has repeated something in her waking day for sixty years, and her consciousness was trying to tell her something about it. The dreaming mind will not give up on telling the dreamer something important about waking life.

Remembering to Remember

A woman dreamt that her own dream images were coming to her from the sky. They were literally falling on her, coming at her from all directions, and she was absorbing them into her body. The sensation was very pleasant, and she enjoyed watching them fall into her.

The first step to remembering dreams is to think about them in waking day. It's good practice to think about previous dreams several times throughout the day. Even if the dreams are very short, thinking about them and remembering that they were dreams is important. This can be done at several intervals throughout the day and just for a few minutes. This begins the process of triggering thoughts about dreams. When thoughts about dreams become important, then dreams themselves will become important to the conscious mind.

The second step is to tell the mind to "remember dreams." Repeating this in a sentence or two, such as "I am remembering my dreams" or "Upon waking, I remember a dream" several times through the waking day will also trigger the conscious mind to remember dreams.

The third step is to think about dreaming as the last thought before going to sleep. Having the mind think about dreams and wanting to remember dreams will greatly be enhanced by making this the last conscious waking thought each night. This in itself will trigger the mind to remember some of the dreams from REM sleep. Once the mind has been primed to remember dreams, it will do exactly that. Now the images need to be recorded and collected in order to be useful for interpretation.

When a woman dreams that dream images are falling from the sky and being absorbed into her body, she is clearly focusing on her dreams. This dream is telling her about her dreams. This imagery tells her that her dreams make her feel good, that they are coming to her, and that she is now getting them. Dreaming about dreams is fairly common when people begin focusing on them and making them important.

Have a System

A young woman dreams about being out with her best friend. This friend is a young man that she has known for many years and considers him to be her closest and dearest friend. In the dream, they are talking and laughing as they often do in waking life. Suddenly, he looks into her eyes, and they embrace in a long and passionate kiss. Upon waking, dream interpretation of this imagery makes her realize that she is actually in love with this man, and her feelings for him have developed far deeper than just friendship.

Once dreams are remembered, then keeping a record of them is very important. The first reason for documenting dreams is that dream interpretation always begins with

TERESA L. DECICCO

recording the dream. The second reason is that a dream may not make sense at all upon waking. The dreamer may not do any dream interpretation thinking that the dream is not that important. After a few days, the imagery may become clear and begin making sense, or another dream may indicate that the previous dream was important. For example, a man dreams that he is picking up money from a muddy lake. He records the dream but does not interpret it. He can't imagine why he would be having this dream since his financial situation is so good. Several nights later, he dreams that his son has lost all his money and is hiding this from his father. He now interprets both dreams about money to gain insight into his relationship with his son. If he did not record the first dream, then the important information about his son would have been lost.

Keeping a dream journal is the best way to keep a record of one's dreams. That is, a separate book just for dreams should be kept, so upon waking, the dream can be recorded. The journal should be kept beside the bed so it is handy to access upon waking. Recording of dreams should become a habit, which then makes this easy to do and requires minimal time.

When recording a dream, it is best to write as much detail as possible, especially if the dream is short. Short dreams can carry as much if not more important information than long ones. Along with dream details, any emotions felt or sensed in the dream should also be recorded.

In order to trigger the conscious mind to remember dreams, it's good to look at some of the dreams before going to bed. At the very least, look at the journal and remind yourself to record any dreams that you can remember. By focusing on dreams and the dream journal and thinking about dreams before sleeping, this increases the likelihood that dreams will be remembered upon waking.

The young woman who dreams of kissing her best friend realizes the deeper emotions that lie within the unconscious. Dream interpretation has helped her with this realization, and now she can begin to make decisions in waking life based on this truth.

Get to Know Your Dreams

A woman reports that her dreams are so long that she feels exhausted to even think about them. The dreams are filled with characters, action, colors, and varied emotions. A man reports that his dreams are always short and vivid and only seem to occur in the middle of the night. When he remembers a dream, it's because the dream has woken him up. A young boy dreams several nights in a row and then doesn't remember any dreams for a long time.

Dream recall varies with each dreamer, so what is considered "normal" is what each dreamer comes to know as his or her own dreaming pattern. People who focus on their dreams more in waking day will have more dream recall. People who are anxious or in highly stressful situations tend to have increased dream recall as well. The key to journaling is that the actual dreaming pattern for the dreamer will be revealed. People may find that they have increased dream recall at certain periods. The quality of dreams will also become apparent as more and more dreams are collected.

One quality that may appear is the amount of color in dreams. Some people dream with very vivid and varied color and others with little or no color. Also, monochromatic or black-and-white dreams are also common for some people. The amount of color can vary, but what is most important about color is what it means to the dreamer. Dream interpretation with color can provide valuable insight that should not be overlooked.

Some people have very long and vivid dreams while others have short and clear dreams. What is important about the quality and quantity of dreams is that dreamers are encouraged to discover their own dream patterns. This is best done with proper dream journaling. In time, the patterns themselves will be useful and will alert the dreamer to specific life events. For example, a series of frightening dreams will alert the dreamer to a stressor in waking life, or a specific image such as a bear or snake may signal danger in waking life. The patterns themselves are filled with information and valuable insights.

CHAPTER 4
DISCOVERING DISCOVERY

Private, Personal, and Confidential Matters

A man dreams that he is dating a woman but finds himself attracted to the woman's brother. In the dream, he is at a family function, and the brother approaches him. He says that he would like to be in a romantic relationship with him and that he should dump his sister. They embrace tenderly and secretly agree to have a relationship without the sister knowing.

Consciousness is a continuous state that flows freely and constantly through an individual both in waking day and in sleep. The mind is busy and active in the waking state and then, during sleep, continues to process information and create meaningful and profound insights while sleeping. The sleeping mind is indeed dynamic and creative. Dreams reveal the lifetime of thoughts, emotions, memories, and experiences that are creating the life of the dreamer, so embedded in this information is the most private and confidential inner self of the individual. It goes without saying that this information must remain protected and should only be revealed to others if the dreamer decides to do so. Given this, all dream interpretation techniques should provide an element of "safety" that will provide meaning and insight without revealing any personal, private, or confidential information to anyone but the dreamer.

It is important to note here that all the techniques provided in this book have a safety element. This ensures that dreamers can be assured that their private information will not be revealed to others and that they always feel safe when working with dreams. By providing safety, then the full value of dreams can be accessed without fear or apprehension.

Information about one's romantic relationships or attractions is generally very private and not shared with others. In the case of a man being attracted to another man in a dream, this is certainly information that could be explored further with dream interpretation. Whatever the meaning for him, he may not want to share it with others. In this case and with all dreams, only techniques that offer complete safety to the dreamer should be used.

Safety

A young woman dreams that she is about to give birth to her first baby. Her husband is present, and they are in the delivery room. She feels herself giving birth to a baby though there is no pain. The doctor announces that the baby is a healthy boy and then places the baby on her chest. Both she and her husband look at the baby and suddenly realize he looks exactly like her ex-boyfriend, the man she was dating when she met her husband. Both she and her husband look at the baby and feel shocked, but neither says a word.

The safety element in dream interpretation must always be active to ensure that dream information is not shared with others unless one chooses to do so. As stated previously, all the techniques that will be covered in this book provide a strong element of safety; that is, all private, personal, and confidential information is kept to the dreamer. Most importantly, all the dream interpretation techniques ensure that insights or imagery are not shared with others and *do not need to be* in order for meanings to become evident to the dreamer. Sharing is always optional.

The first method, The Storytelling Method of Dream Interpretation, uses a worksheet to lead the dreamer from dream imagery to waking day insights. The Worksheet is a self-directed dream therapy technique, which means the dreamer works through the dream without having to share the information with others, including a therapist. Therapists and clinicians who use the Worksheet do so in groups and in private sessions, but either way, it is still the dreamer who works through the steps toward insight and, again, never having to share information about the dream or insight unless he or she chooses to do so.

A Worksheet is also used for the second method, which is the 2A Method. With this method, deep emotions from the dream and waking life are evoked. This Worksheet is a technique that provides complete safety whether it is used in groups, private therapy sessions, or in self-directed dream work.

The third technique called the Projective Method is a group-sharing technique. That is, one person tells a dream to others, and the group then helps the dreamer find meaning and insight into the dream. This method, though it involves group sharing, also provides safety since the dreamer never has to reveal if any insights or meanings surface. The dreamer keeps all information about revelations to himself or herself. The dreamer does, however, have to report a dream to the group, so only dreams that one feels comfortable sharing should be shared. Complete safety is encouraged with this method so that the deepest and most private information of the dreamer is protected.

Finally, the last technique is Meditative Dream Re-Entry, which takes the dreamer into the deepest level of meaning for a dream. This technique allows the dreamer to let the dream imagery and meanings unfold without having to share them in any way. Since the deepest and most personal information is revealed with this method, it is especially important that the dreamer feel safe when working with it. The method can be used in a group session or in group therapy, then safety is again ensured since the entire technique is kept private for each dreamer. Group members can follow the directions, allow the technique to guide them to their dream's meaning, and feel safe while doing so.

In summary, safety is one of the most important elements of dream interpretation. This element protects the dreamer, protects the dream images, and keeps the most pertinent information secured—that is, the dream's true meaning.

The young woman who dreams of giving birth to her ex-boyfriend's baby and not her husband's baby comes to terms with her infidelity in her marriage. She has been hiding the fact that she is seeing another man, and this has come to the surface of consciousness in her dreams. This private, confidential, and personal information must be protected in dream interpretation as she decides how to deal with it in her waking life.

Discovery

A woman dreams that she is in her current home and looking out the kitchen window. Instead of seeing her yard, she sees a vast field covered in yellow flowers. The view is so beautiful, it brings her to tears.

When working with dreams the second most important element is "discovery" for the dreamer. That is, when the dreamer connects the dream to some aspect of his or her own life or when a meaning or insight has occurred. This can look and feel like an instant "aha" moment or can develop over time when working with the dream in waking day. The dreamer feels that the insight or discovery clearly makes sense in terms of waking life or waking life circumstances. The purpose of this book is to lead the dreamer to these "aha" moments with several dream interpretation techniques. Once this happens, the dreamer can then assimilate the discovery into waking day circumstances and really begin living life fully.

A dreamer who dreams about a garden of yellow flowers may be led to the discovery that she longs to go back to a neighborhood she lived in with her partner before he died. She may discover further that she was never really happy in the place she now lives. The dreamer can then explore the waking day circumstances that surround this situation. She may reconcile where she currently lives, explore moving back to where she previously lived, or explore moving to a completely new neighborhood. It is constructive dream interpretation that will lead the dreamer to new insights, new avenues, and possibly new solutions for life situations. The key to dream interpretation is learning and practicing dream interpretation techniques that will lead dreamers to these often life-changing discoveries.

Not Discovering Discovery

A man dreams that he is eating a sandwich and suddenly finds one of his own teeth in the sandwich. He discovers that the tooth has just fallen out. He takes another bite of the sandwich and then loses another tooth into the sandwich. This keeps happening until all his teeth have fallen out.

57

Not every dream interpretation method will lead to discovery, and there are several reasons for this. First, not everyone will enjoy using all four dream interpretation techniques. That means for methods that do not resonate with the dreamer, the method may not be used fully or with enthusiasm. Given this, the meaning will not arise when the dreamer is not fully engaged with the method. Second, each method leads to a different level of meaning. If a dream is literally about a waking day circumstance (e.g., it is telling a dreamer to get a new job because the boss is abusive) and a method is used to look for a deeper, hidden meaning, there may not be one there. The meaning is directly related to waking life, and there is nothing else to be had from it. Dreamers must become aware of when to use which method. Third, the dreamer may have a blind spot and not see the meaning, even when the interpretation methods reveal it. A blind spot occurs when the meaning is presented, but the dreamer does not want to see it or accept it. For example, The Storytelling Method may reveal that a dreamer should leave his current job. If he is not willing to "see" this discovery, then he may believe he has not found the meaning. These blind spots can be a problem because even when discovery is revealed, the dreamer does not want to see that discovery has been revealed. One solution is to use more than one method, and then the same message of discovery may be hard to ignore. If The Storytelling Method reveals that a man should leave his current job and then the 2A Method reveals this as well, he may find it hard to ignore this truth. If he does one or two more methods with the dream and gets this same or similar message, then it will be even harder to ignore. So if an interpretation does not initially appear to lead to discovery, then different methods may either get to the actual meaning or unblock the blind spot.

Each technique in this book offers a unique method that will lead to different levels of discovery or meaning. For example, The Storytelling Method may reveal that a man should leave his current job because the boss is abusive. The 2A Method may reveal the emotions of pain and anguish that he is suppressing at work when the boss is being abusive. The Projective Method may reveal that his work situation is one that is literally unhealthy for him, and finally, Meditative Dream Re-Entry may reveal that his boss is similar to his abusive father and that leaving his job finds him happy and healthy again. Each technique contributes an important and unique element to his situation and to his life.

This book provides a system of dream interpretation and suggests that each technique be used in the order that it is taught because each method builds on the next and may provide a new level of discovery. Each technique will provide a different level of meaning, depending on the imagery that is being worked with. Another example to illustrate how each technique contributes uniquely to discovery is that the Storytelling Method may reveal to a dreamer that a dream is about a current day romantic relationship. This method brings into conscious awareness that the current romantic relationship is a problem. The 2A Method may then provide the emotion that is coming up for the dreamer, which may be boredom and emptiness in the relationship. The Projective Method may then provide more insights such as how bad it feels to be in the relationship and possible solutions to the situation. Finally, Meditative Dream Re-Entry provides the deepest and most intimate longings of the ideal relationship, which looks and feels very differently than the current one. Each method can add something different and meaningful to the discovery process. Since dreams appear in the mind as images that are connected in many complex ways to the dreamer's life, different dream interpretations help to connect those complexities and reveal the innermost mysteries of one's life—the mysteries of relationships, happiness, life long passions, success, and how to ultimately cultivate the waking life of one's dreams.

Dreams of one's own teeth falling out are quite common. The dream interpretation methods will lead the dreamer to finding out what this imagery means specifically for them. For example, it may mean that waking day stressors are triggering this imagery or that someone is avoiding a much needed dentist appointment in waking day. Either way, the meaning can be revealed with dream interpretation that will be helpful to the dreamer's own life.

CHAPTER 5
THE STORYTELLING METHOD OF DREAM INTERPRETATION

The Dream Tells a Story

A woman dreams that she is at her beautiful home with a man that she is dating. They are standing on her deck embracing and kissing each other. Suddenly her ex-husband walks in and interrupts them. The woman goes into her house to get her son so he can go with his dad. She looks around, and her home is now old and shabby. She then looks at herself in the mirror and discovers she is aged, very obese, and covered in wrinkles.

Human culture has recognized the importance of storytelling since the beginning of time. Stories have been conveyed by pictures on cave walls, on ancient tablets, or in the form of fairytales. In our modern society, stories continue to play an important role in our lives through movies, plays, books, and other mediums. One way dreams can be interpreted is that they too are telling us stories that relate to ourselves and our lives.

Dreams appear in the mind as images that are connected in many complex ways to the dreamer's life. These images can be taken with The Storytelling Method (TSM) and be constructively linked to waking day circumstances, events, and the dreamer in many ways in the form of a story. By using the TSM Worksheet provided and explained in this chapter, the dream becomes a story relevant to the dreamer with revelations that directly link to waking day circumstances.

TSM is a dream interpretation method that was scientifically designed and tested by the author of this book in order to reveal the story that a dream may be telling. This method has been proven to be very useful in many important ways.

First, TSM has been found to significantly lead to discovery. That means that the method, when conducted with the worksheet provided, leads the dreamer to meaning and insight, more often than when the worksheet is not used. It was found that the worksheet provides a structure that guides the dreamer to create a meaningful story from the dream. The premise of the method is that it is based on two guiding principles: writing out the dream and then making associations from words and phrases from the dream. The next step, which is to create a personal story from the associations, is the unique and guiding factor. Research has shown that people have more insight and meaning from the dream once they have created the story than if they just do word association alone.

As discussed in chapter 4, safety is a very important element in dream interpretation. TSM provides safety so private and confidential material is not revealed to others. The worksheet is provided in the Appendix of this book, so it can be copied and placed in one's dream journal. The worksheet is a self-guided dream interpretation technique, so complete confidentiality is assured.

Therapists and dream workers alike favor TSM because it is easy to use and not time consuming. The method is practical so people can use it on a regular basis without much interruption in their day. Since it is so practical, it has been found that people tend to use it for long periods of time, and therefore, it makes dream interpretation that much more beneficial. Though long and detailed methods of dream interpretation may be useful and interesting, people tend not to comply with them for long because they are just not practical. The aim of TSM is to have a method that is practical, useful, user-friendly, but most importantly, leads to significant discoveries.

As a dream therapy, TSM has been shown to be useful for insight and guidance for a wide range of people. Women suffering from breast cancer have used this method and found that they are able to find substantial meaning from their dreams. This is particularly important since people suffering from cancer tend to have dreams with negative, anxious, and fearful imagery. The meanings derived from the dreams were directly related to their health and to other waking day situations. It was found that discoveries from TSM helped them cope with waking day life.

TSM has also been used with people suffering from physical pain and was also found to be extremely constructive. The stories that emerged helped them cope with waking day situations that their pain directly affected, such as treatment methods, relationships, family dynamics, or employment situations.

People in romantic relationships who use TSM as an interpretation method also report that is it very useful for insight into their relationships. The method often exposed underlying emotions or problems causing negativity or relationship tribulations. The method was also found useful since solutions to relationship problems or possible directions for solving waking day issues were often revealed.

Alcoholics and drug and food addicts often use TSM for coping with addictions. Interestingly, TSM is useful and powerful for tapping into the circumstances related to the addictions. Insight into the addictions and the underlying causes of the addiction are revealed in the personal stories created with the method. Often surprising to the dreamers, the real issue of addiction is portrayed in the stories created.

All of these cases and many others have shown that The Storytelling Method leads to discovery, insight, and provides valuable information to the dreamer about life circumstances. The purpose of the storytelling method is to bridge dream imagery to waking day circumstances for the dreamer, and it has shown to do just that.

TSM is always a good starting point to working with any dream, and each step of the method will be outlined in detail in this chapter. Appendix A has a blank copy of the worksheet for participants to photocopy and add to their dream journal as needed.

The woman who has a dream about suddenly aging discovers with TSM that she needs to forgive her ex-husband. The method helps her discover that events from her past are keeping her stuck there and preventing her from moving on. The dream is not only a mechanism for helping her move from her past but also a mechanism for helping to create a better relationship in her future.

The Storytelling Method (TSM)

This method was designed in order to get people started on dream interpretation with a systematic method that is easy to use, not time consuming, provides discovery easily and quickly, and would be safe for dreamers to use while leading them to important discoveries. There are five steps to the method, and they must *all* be followed in order for discovery to occur. Also, it is very important that they be used *in the order* that they appear. Research on TSM has shown that the method works best with the worksheet that is provided and presented in this book. After following each step as directed, important discoveries are likely to occur for the dreamer.

Step 1

In Step 1 of TSM the directions state to write out the dream in the space provided.

The instructions are as follows:

Write your dream in the space below. Write in full sentences and with as much detail as possible.

This is a very important step since this is the basis for working with the dream. It is important to write the dream out in as much detail as possible and add any emotions that are remembered. Other important details include colors, sensations, sounds, or smells. Any details are important, no matter how small they seem. If someone is dreaming about something, it is surely important to them.

The second important step here is to *only* work with one dream scene at a time, particularly if the dream is long. That is, when a dream changes scenes such as a location or storyline, then that is considered a new dream scene. For example, when a dreamer dreams a long scene with a group of people sitting on a beach all interacting with each other, then that is one dream scene. If suddenly the dream shifts so the dreamer finds himself in a stranger's house and running to hide in the basement, then that is another scene. Each dream scene will provide a specific meaning or insight for the dreamer. If TSM is used with a very long dream that contains several scenes, the meaning of each scene may be lost. It is especially important to remember that one dream may have several meanings, and therefore working with each scene may provide valuable insight at several levels. Step 1 is the first step in dream interpretation, which is to record the dream in detail, and preferably, just upon waking.

Example of Step 1

My boyfriend and I are asleep in my bed. The light is either on, or it is daytime. I wake up to something falling on me. It's a huge spider. I scream and jump out of the bed and wake up my boyfriend. At this point, I notice there are spiders all over the ceiling. My mom comes into the room because of the screaming and sees the spiders. She isn't afraid and starts killing the spiders right away. When she kills them they just disappear. She decides we should take the sheets off my bed, and as we are doing this, the spiders start crawling out of my mattress and I realize I was sleeping on them the whole time.

This is a good example of a recorded dream. She has recorded enough detail so dream interpretation should be fairly straightforward. The dream includes just one dream scene, so the message from this scene should emerge as the steps are followed.

Step 2

In Step 2, the dreamer chooses the most important or "salient" words in the dream. The instructions are as follows:

Go back to the dream on the previous page and underline the most important or "salient" word or phrase for you in each sentence.

The most important feature here is that the dreamer go over each sentence and choose the words that are the most important for him or her. It is the dreamer who decides what words are most meaningful or significant, and these words will then guide the interpretation method. Whatever word or phrase or words that stand out the most in each sentence are the words chosen, as in the following example.

Example of Step 2

My boyfriend and I are <u>asleep</u> in my bed. The light is either on, or it is <u>daytime</u>. I wake up to something <u>falling on me</u>. It's a huge <u>spider</u>. I <u>scream</u> and jump out of the bed and wake up my boyfriend. At this point, I notice there are spiders all over the <u>ceiling</u>. My mom comes into the room because of the screaming and sees the <u>spiders</u>. She isn't afraid and starts <u>killing the spiders</u> right away. When she kills them they just <u>disappear</u>. She decides we should take the sheets off my bed, and as we are doing this, the spiders start <u>crawling out</u> of my mattress and I realize I was sleeping on them the whole time.

The dreamer chooses the words by how important they are, or how they resonate with him or her. This step does not require much thought or contemplation. The important words will appear fairly obvious since they cause an emotional shift or stirring for the dreamer. Once the words or phrases are underlined, then Step 3(a) of TSM can be carried out.

Step 3(a)

The instructions are as follows:

Write the underlined words in the order that they appear in the dream in Section A below.

This step involves simply taking the underlined words or phrases from Step 2 and writing them in a table format. The table is provided on the TSM Worksheet, and the words are written under Section A of the sheet. The important steps here are the following:

1. The words must be written **in the order** that they appear in the dream.

2. The words must not be changed or reworded. The words from the dream must appear in the table as they are in the dream (no paraphrasing).

3. Words must not be omitted from the list. All the words and phrases that were underlined in the dream must appear in the list.

Example of Step 3(a)

Section A	**Section B**
Asleep	
Daytime	

Falling on me

Spider

Scream

Ceiling

Spiders

Killing the spiders

Disappear

Crawling out

It is very important to simply transcribe the words as they appear and in the same order. This maintains the integrity of the dream and keeps all salient or important dream elements cohesive for the next step.

Step 3(b)

Step 3(b) is the association step of interpretation. That means for each word in Section A then a corresponding association is written in Section B. Instructions are as follows:

Go back to the table on page 2 and put down in Section B the first word that comes to mind for you for each word in Section A.

Associations should be made one word at a time and fairly quickly. The first word that comes to mind for each word in Section A should then be written in Section B. Very little thought should be given in the association process, but rather, the first word or feeling that comes to mind is the correct one.

For the example we have been working through, the first word in Section A is "asleep." The associated word for this by the dreamer is "peaceful." That means that this is the first word that comes to mind for the dreamer when she reads "asleep." Every person will have a different association for the word "asleep" because the association is unique to the dreamer's own life. The completed association list for Step 3(b) looks like this:

Example:

Section A	**Section B**
Asleep	Peaceful
Daytime	Sunny
Falling on me	Hurt
Spider	Black and hairy
Scream	Scared
Ceiling	Roof
Spiders	Unsafe
Killing the spiders	Safe
Disappear	Go away
Crawling out	Unsafe

The list of words from Section B are now the associated words that emerged from the dream. That is, the dream images were created in the sleeping mind, and now those important images and words are being converted into the conscious waking mind with associations. This is an important step because the conscious waking mind can now take the dream images and make sense of them. The words emerge into a conscious story in Step 4 of TSM.

Step 4

In this step the words from Section B are linked together to form a meaningful story to the dreamer. Instructions state:

Take the words in Section B and write a short and simple story with the words. Keep the words <u>in the order that they appear</u> in the list. The story should make sense to you.

The story should be one that connects the words in a way that makes sense to the dreamer. Each word can create one sentence, or the words may link together such that two or three words are in once sentence. However the words are connected, they should be meaningful to the dreamer. Each sentence then builds on the previous one so the story unfolds.

For example, the words in Section B may be *cat, follow, sad, me*. The story that unfolds from these words may be the following:

My cat tended to follow me around. I am sad that she died because I am left alone now. It's just me.

Another example may be the words *swallow, Tom, child, my life, light.* The story from these words may be the following:

It's hard to swallow the fact that Tom left me. He is having a child now with someone else. I know my life will be better. I just need to see the light.

The stories that emerge are as unique as is the life of each dreamer. The stories are created from the mind, emotions, and experiences of the dreamer and, therefore, will be created from the dreamer's mind for the dreamer. The important features of Step 4 are the following:

1) The story should make sense to the dreamer. More than one attempt at creating a story may have to occur before a meaningful story emerges.

2) All the words from Section B must be included in the story.

3) The words must be kept in the order that they appear in the list.

4) Only words from Section B are included in the story (none from Section A).

5) Only the dreamer can create the story for him or herself. No one else can really know the life of the dreamer and how the words can be connected in a meaningful way.

From our example in Step 1, the following story emerged from the dreamer:

It was a peaceful and sunny day when I got very hurt. The black and hairy monster of a man scared me. I wanted to run to the roof because I was so unsafe. In

order to feel safe again I had to go away. I never want to feel unsafe again.

This story that emerged connected the words in a meaningful way. Steps 5 a–d then help the dreamer to connect the story to any waking life situations that might be arising.

Step 5(a)

The instructions for this step are as follows:

Does the story having meaning for you? Explain.

When asking this question, the dreamer tries to connect the story to any memories or situations that come to mind. Often the story has some connection, if vaguely, to thoughts, feelings, or waking life circumstances. For the example from Step 5 above, the question was answered in the following way:

Example of 5(a):

Yes. This reminds me of a situation I had one night while I was out with me friends.

Step 5 (b)

The question of this step helps the dreamer to further connect the story to waking life. This question helps the dreamer to think directly about waking life circumstances:

Does this story relate to your waking life in some way? Explain.

Thinking about waking life circumstances directly will help to evoke further any thoughts, feelings, or connections to the story. This will often expand the story's meaning to help the dreamer get further into the dream.

Example of 5(b):

This story relates directly to a night I was out at a club with my friends. A man who seemed very dark and mean approached me. When I shunned him, he became angry and that scared me. I just wanted to get out of there because I felt so unsafe around him.

Step 5(c)

This step asks the dreamer to get further into the story and a possible meaning. By asking about a "specific" event, this may trigger other thoughts and feelings for the dreamer. Step 5(c) asks the following question:

Does this story relate to any <u>specific events</u> in your waking life?

In our example from above, the question is answered in 5(c).

Example of 5(c):

Yes. My dad scared me when I was a child because he would get violently angry if he didn't get what he wanted from us. The man in the club reminded me that people like my father scare me. I don't want to be around them.

Step 5(d)

This question asks the dreamer to think about "insight." This means trying to connect the story and the meaning of the story to a life situation. This extends the meaning past the story itself into other areas of one's life. The question states:

Did this analysis give you any clear insight? Yes_____ No _____

If the answer is yes, then the dreamer can think about other situations that relate to the story in Step 5(e).

Step 5(e):

If yes, write about the insight and how it relates to your life.

The purpose of insight and discovery is to then make changes in waking life. This is the most useful process of any dream interpretation technique. The TSM worksheets should be kept in the dream journal and read over occasionally in the weeks and months ahead of the dream. This will remind the dreamer of the insights gained and help to guide behavior in waking day.

If the answer is "no" to question 5(d), that is, no insight emerged, then TSM can be repeated at another time with the same dream, or another dream interpretation method can be used. One technique will not work for every dream, and therefore, several techniques are useful in any dream interpretation program.

The next section of this book is to guide dreamers through TSM with a dream. Spaces are provided in order to work through each step until the method and discovery become comfortable. A blank copy of TSM is provided in Appendix A for future use with more dreams.

Working Through a Dream: The Storytelling Method

Step 1

Write your dream in the space below. Write in full sentences and with as much detail as possible.

Step 2

Go back to the dream on the previous page and underline the most important or "salient" word or phrase for you in each sentence.

Step 3(a) Write the underlined words in the order that they appear in the dream in Section A below:

Section A   **Section B**

Step 3(b) Go back to the table on the previous page and put down in Section B the first word that comes to mind for you for each word in Section A.

Step 4

Take the words in Section B and write a short and simple story with the words. Keep the words <u>in the order that they appear</u> in the list. The story should make sense to you.

Step 5

Answer the following questions:

a) Does this story have meaning for you? Explain.

b) Does this story relate to your waking life in some way? Explain.

d) Does this story relate to any <u>specific events</u> in your waking life?

e) Did this analysis give you any clear insight? ____ yes ____ no

e) If yes, write about the insight and how it relates to your life.

CHAPTER 6
GETTING EMOTIONAL

The Emotional Map

A man dreams that he is in an old building and realizes it was his high school. He has been left with the keys to lock up, but someone breaks in while he is packing up to leave. The police come and tell him that a trap has been set and a bomb is about to go off. He looks for a way to escape, but he cannot get out and doesn't know exactly where he is.

One of the most important elements shared by all of human kind is the active emotional life within. People all over the world fall in love, grieve losses, feel anger at injustices, rejoice with successes, and indulge in joy when they can. The emotions of humans are often as mysterious and distinct as is each individual. Though most people share the same emotions to some extent such as fear, anger, and love, the degree and resonance of these emotions is completely unique within each person. One's emotional life defines, expresses, and illustrates personality, life experiences, and ultimately character.

Emotions are one of the most important sources of information for people. Feelings of joy signal that one is in a place in life that is positive and good. Feelings of joy when with a particular person, signals that this is the right person to be with. Feelings of excitement or contentment with one's work signal that the job is the correct one for that person. Similarly, feelings of peacefulness or joy when doing a leisure activity such as playing tennis or riding a bike means that activity should be engaged in. Therefore, positive emotions are a gauge and guide to the positive directions of one's life.

Negative emotions and emotional pain are important signals that something is wrong with one's life. For example, feeling sad or depressed with one's work is a sign that a job is not one that you should be engaged in. Feeling angry or generally uncomfortable with a person indicates something is wrong with the relationship. Negative feelings, just like positive ones, should be used as a guide to move toward or away from an event or others.

Sometimes emotions send confusing signals that get misread. For example, when someone feels desperately lonely, they may begin drinking too much alcohol to numb the pain. The feeling may be read that alcohol makes one feel better, but in reality, the loneliness needs to be addressed and not masked. Emotions, when attended to, can be an internal map so to speak, guiding one toward positive and good things in life and away from painful or negative things.

Even though emotions are essential and basic to the human condition, people often become quite disconnected from their own emotional source. When this occurs, a disconnection from the internal guidance that steers people toward positive things and away from negative things in life occurs. The emotional life can also become confused, distorted, and convoluted with mixed emotions. The true emotions at the heart of the dreamer, however, never get completely shut off because the unconscious continues to process them. This being the case, dreams will convey important information about the emotional life of the dreamer. In fact, many researchers and clinicians believe that the emotions actually drive the dreams themselves. Tapping into the emotions in dreams will reveal vital information about the dreamer and life circumstances; often this information is completely unknown to the dreamer.

Feelings of being trapped or lost in dreams are very important elements that can be linked to waking day events. If one is willing to work with their own emotions and tap into the events that trigger them, then great life changes can occur. A dream about a bomb going off and being trapped may trigger a "ticking time bomb" in waking life that needs to be addressed.

Unearthing Emotions

A man dreams that he is walking around a grocery store when the lights suddenly go out. The store is very dark, and he cannot see his way. The lights then come on, and the store is completely empty except for a little girl about five years of age standing at the end of the empty room. The girl does not say a word, but she is very sad and very troubled.

Getting to the emotional state of an individual is often difficult and confusing. Emotions get tangled together, get misread (e.g., am I really angry or am I in love?), and generally get harder and harder to access over time.

One dream interpretation technique that was designed to examine the emotional currents of dreams is the 2A Method. This method guides the dreamer to make associations from a dream and then to amplify the associations, especially with emotions attached to each association. The feelings around important and salient dream symbols become apparent with the 2A Method. The next chapter will discuss and illustrate the method while the Appendix has a copy of the method that can be photocopied for future use.

Emotions are a very important element in creating one's life yet they are often ignored the most. Dreams will bring emotions into the mind for conscious awareness to examine. The emotional level of a dream is often the most important information in life change. The man who dreams of a sad little girl can relate this to his own life or ignore it and continue to create the same waking life patterns.

CHAPTER 7

THE 2A METHOD: ASSOCIATION AND AMPLIFICATION

Tapping into Dream Emotions

Scientific studies have shown that dreams are driven by both the emotional life and the personality of the dreamer in unison. In fact, emotions felt in the waking day and emotions not acknowledged or expressed are kept in the unconscious and become very important in dreams. For example, a woman having romantic feelings for a married man may keep those feelings in the unconscious mind but they may show up in the dreaming mind. The 2A Method of dream interpretation helps to access the emotions in dreams and then leads to discovering what those dream images mean. This method is the next logical step from The Storytelling Method since it will reveal the emotions that drive the events that are creating the dream images.

Step 1: Write Out Your Dream

Using the 2A Method Worksheet provided, the first step is to write out the dream as it is remembered. As with The Storytelling Method, as much detail as possible is included. If the dream is long, then each dream scene is interpreted separately with a separate worksheet, as each scene will contain a separate and important message. A dream scene is when the dream imagery shifts dramatically in location, emotion, or major story line. For example in a dream a woman is running down a street as she is being chased by a giant rhinoceros. She is feeling afraid but thinking that rhinos probably don't eat people. She runs through narrow streets and darts traffic but can sense that the rhino is still following her. Even though the rhino is very large, it seems to fit in the narrow streets and has no trouble following her. Suddenly, she runs into an old school friend whom she recognizes. She and the friend are now standing in a mall talking about a mutual childhood friend and the dream continues. This dream is considered to be in two dream scenes since they are in two separate locations and have different emotions attached to them. The instructions for Step 1 in the 2A Method are as follows:

In the space below write your dream as you remember it. Include as much detail as possible. If you have several dream scenes, then record each scene on a separate worksheet and interpret each scene separately.

Example of Step 1

Two guys kidnapped me. I tried to escape by running away. Both guys pulled out guns on me, and I could feel the pressure. I got really scared and begged for my life back. Finally, my roommate grabbed my arm when she was walking back from a coffee shop. We ran across the street and hid in the bushes. I was hoping to be safe. Suddenly, my roommate screamed and I screamed. The guy caught my foot, and I woke up in a panic.

This is a good dream for the 2A Method because there is a strong emotional element in this dream. Clearly this dreamer has fear about something that is driving this imagery. The fact that the strong emotions woke her up in a panic indicates that the 2A Method may reveal something important for her.

Step 2: Key Words and Phrases

As with The Storytelling Method, the 2A Method requires that key words and phrases be underlined in the dream. Ten to fifteen words or phrases are chosen from the dream; these are words that stand out or are particularly salient for the dreamer. Instructions state the following:

Go back to your dream on the previous page and circle or underline up to ten or fifteen key words or phrases that stand out for you. If you have more than 10–15 words, you can put those on another worksheet.

Example of Step 2:

Two guys <u>kidnapped</u> me. I tried to <u>escape</u> by running away. Both guys <u>pulled</u> out <u>guns</u> on me, and I could feel the <u>pressure</u>. I got really <u>scared</u> and <u>begged</u> for my <u>life</u> back. Finally, my <u>roommate</u> grabbed my arm when she was walking back from <u>the coffee shop</u>. We ran across the <u>street</u> and <u>hid</u> in the <u>bushes</u>. I was <u>hoping</u> to be safe. Suddenly, my roommate <u>screamed</u> and I screamed. The guy caught my foot, and I woke up in a panic.

Step 2(a): Words and Associations

In this step, the words and phrases that were underlined in the dream are then written in Column A of the worksheet. The instructions are as follows:

Take the words that you circled or underlined and write them in **Column A** below. Keep the words <u>in the order that they appear</u> in the dream.

Example of Step 2(a):

Column A   **Column B**

Kidnapped

Escape

Pulled

Guns

Pressure

Scared

Begged

Life

Roommate

The coffee shop

Street

Hid

Bushes

Hoping

Screamed

Step 2(b)

This step involves making associations from the words chosen from the dream:

Write in Column B below the first word that comes to mind for each word in Column A. Keep the words in the order that they appear.

Example of 2(b):

Column A	Column B
Kidnapped	Scared
Escape	Desperate
Pulled	Forced
Guns	End
Pressure	Fast
Scared	Fear
Begged	Wanted
Life	Complicated
Roommate	Friendly
Tim Hortons	Work
Street	Closed
Hid	Embarrassed
Bushes	Green
Hoping	Pray
Screamed	Doomed

The important factor in this step is to keep the words in the order that they appear in the dream. Therefore, the associations in Column B are kept in order as well.

Step 3: Amplification

Step 3 is a larger worksheet that is followed through in three steps across the worksheet. In 3(a), the instructions are

1) Write the words from Column B in the order they appear in Section 1 below.

In 3b, the instructions are

2) Fill in Section 2 by answering the questions below.

The questions allow amplification to occur and guide the dreamer to expand and amplify each salient word from Section 1. The questions to answer for each word are the following:

What does this word remind you of?

How is this word related to you in your life?

Who reminds you of this word in your waking life?

Where are you in relation to this word?

Why does this word relate to you in some way?

The answers to each question are written in Section 2. Section 3(c) then allows for the emotions to be explored from the amplification:

3) Write three emotions that the words in Section 2 remind you of.

It is here that the emotions that surface will be recorded. Further exploration of the words and feelings occur in Step 4 of the interpretation method.

Step 3: Example

Section 1:	*Section 2:*	*Section 3:*
Words	**What does this word remind you of?**	**3 Emotions**
	How is this word related to you in your life?	
	Who reminds you of this word in your waking life?	
	Where are you in relation to this word?	
	Why does this word relate to you in some way?	
Scared	*Myself, scared of risks, me, anywhere, it's about me*	*scared, anxious, confused*
Desperate	*Homeless people, caring for others, homeless, classroom, I'm dedicated*	*pitiful, nervous, sad*
Forced	*A boy, I was forced, this boy, house, it's about me and this boy*	*disgust, shame, upset*
End	*Yellowing, end of teen hood, myself, home, my birthday*	*happy, fear, enjoy*
Fast	*Rabbits, my Chinese sign, myself, home, I'm fast*	*surprise interest, pride*

Fear	Bugs, I'm terrified of bugs, bugs, outside, bees	sad, fear, anger
Wanted	Love, relationship, my boyfriend, my room, it's about me and him	wonder, amusement, happy
Complicated	Life, everything is complicated, myself, everywhere, simple	confused, upset, disappointed
Friendly	Teachers, relationship, Margaret, school, friendliness is a good quality	love, respect, courage
Work	Library, my work, myself work, I work there	happy, bored, courage
Close	Intimately, time with myself, my boyfriend, room, my boyfriend loves me	happy, happy, courage
Embarrassed	My mom, my mom upset and embarrassed, my mother, home, she's insecure	nervous, timid, scared
Green	Parks, fun, my friends, outside, I like to have fun	shy, nervous, fearful
Pray	God, religion, my grandmother, church, my beliefs	hopeful, proud, nervous
Doomed	Dark, I'm afraid, me, inside me, I feel doomed	scared, empty, afraid

Step 4: Insight

This step allows the dreamer to explore the dream from the associations, amplifications, and emotions in several ways.

The first step is to read over the passages written, and the second is to answer the questions asked:

Read over the words from Section 2 and the feelings in Section 3 that are associated with your words. Read this over several times and then answer the following questions:

Do these words and feelings make any sense to you?

Does this relate to you personally in any way?

Do the words and feelings relate to any specific events in your waking life?

Do the words and feelings remind you of anyone else's life situation?

Example of Step 4: Insight

Do these words and feelings make any sense to you?

Yes, they make sense to me because it involves negative feelings/emotions associated with a negative situation I have had in my life.

Does this relate to you personally in any way?

Yes, it relates to me because I feel very negative most of the time. I don't think my relationship with my boyfriend will turn out because of me.

Do the words and feelings relate to any specific events in your waking life?

Yes, I've experienced sexual assault by someone years ago, which explains why I feel so negative.

Do the words and feelings remind you of anyone else's life situation?

Someone once told me that she could not have a healthy relationship with a man until she dealt with her sexual assault. Maybe I need to consider this as well.

Using the 2A Method

The 2A method can be used on the same dream that was interpreted with The Storytelling Method, whether discovery was achieved or not. The Storytelling Method may reveal connections to waking day insights and events that are very helpful and useful. The 2A Method with the same dream may then reveal more information or different information that will be even more useful. For example, a man uses The Storytelling Method and discovers that he is unhappy in his job but is staying for the money and benefits. Discovery with the 2A Method then reveals that he is actually afraid to change his job for fear that he does not have the skills to acquire a new job. It is actually his fear that keeps him in his current job and not the job itself. With this information, he can now begin retraining himself for a new job, choose to stay in his job that makes him unhappy, or find a completely different line of work.

If The Storytelling Method does not reveal discovery for a dream, then the 2A Method can be used to work with the emotions that create and mold the imagery. It may be that a dream does not connect to any concrete waking day events, so The Storytelling Method may not reveal discovery, but if emotions are the key feature of the dream, then the 2A Method will be useful. So if one method does not work, then another may tap into the dream in a different way. This makes several proven dream interpretation methods invaluable in the process of discovery. The following section provides space to interpret a dream with the 2A Method. The same dream can be used as was interpreted with The Storytelling Method, or a new dream can be used for personal insight.

Using the 2A Method with Your Dream

Step 1: Write Out Your Dream

In the space below write your dream as you remember it. Include as much detail as possible. If you have several dream scenes, then record each scene on a separate worksheet and interpret each scene separately

Step 2: Key Words and Phrases

Go back to your dream on the previous page and circle or underline up to ten or fifteen key words or phrases that stand out for you. If you have more than 10–15 words you can put those on another worksheet. Keep the words in the order that they appear.

Step 2(a): Words and Associations

Take the words that you circled or underlined and write them in Column A below. Keep the words <u>in the order that they appear</u> in the dream.

Column A   **Column B**

Step 2(b)

Write in Column B below the first word that comes to mind for each word in Column A. Keep the words in the order that they appear.

Step 3: Amplification

1) Write the words from Column B in the order they appear in Section I on the next page.

2) Fill in Section 2 by answering the questions below.

> What does this word remind you of?
>
> How is this word related to you in your life?
>
> Who reminds you of this word in your waking life?
>
> Where are you in relation to this word?
>
> Why does this word relate to you in some way?

3) Write three emotions in Section 3 that the words in Section 2 remind you of.

The 2A Worksheet

Section 1:	*Section 2:*	*Section 3:*
Words	**What does this word remind you of?**	**3 Emotions**
	How is this word related to you in your life?	
	Who reminds you of this word in your waking life?	
	Where are you in relation to this word?	
	Why does this word relate to you in some way?	

Step 4: Insight

Read over the words from Section 2 and the feelings in Section 3 that are associated with your words. Read this over several times and then answer the following questions:

Do these words and feelings make any sense to you?

Does this relate to you personally in any way?

Do the words and feelings relate to any specific events in your waking life?

Do the words and feelings remind you of anyone else's life situation?

CHAPTER 8
SHARING THE DREAM

It's Nice to Share

A woman dreams that she has just killed her boyfriend and put him in the trunk of her car. She feels nervous and afraid that someone will see what she has done. She drives the car to a nearby fire station and parks it out the back. She then gets out and begins walking calmly away from the car. She is thinking to herself that she is ashamed and embarrassed for what she has done but is also filled with relief.

People generally love to share their dreams with others and have done so from the beginning of time. However, people often don't realize that there is personal, private, and confidential information embedded in dream imagery. When choosing to share dreams with others, it is important that safety be provided. That is, any personal information about the dreamer's own life must remain protected. Group-sharing methods of dream interpretation teach people to share their dreams while providing possible discovery to the dreamer; however, the dreamer never has to reveal any revelations about waking life or any information whatsoever to others in the group. This is a great way for friends, family, and dream groups to share their dreams and insights with each other.

In many cultures, sharing dreams with others is a common, everyday practice. Also, people just like to tell others about their dreams, even if they don't want to analyze or interpret them at all. Sharing dreams seems to have, in itself, a very useful purpose.

Given this, several professionals have designed techniques based on dream sharing. Some techniques are designed for the clinical setting where a therapist or professional leads a group into helping someone with a dream. Others are more informal but are designed for groups of people to share their dreams and provide guidance to meaningful insights.

The next chapter will discuss a method of dream sharing that is used in group therapy, workshops, and informal settings. The method provides a technique so that sharing can occur among family members, friends, co-workers, or any other group of people interested in doing dream interpretation together. The method has been tested and found to lead to discovery while providing safety for the dreamer.

When a woman dreams that she has killed her boyfriend and hidden him in the trunk of her car, feelings and events around the relationship are explored with the group sharing method. While sharing this dream she discovers that she is very unhappy in the relationship and wants it to secretly be terminated. While hearing the input from others in her group, she discovers that the relationship is "killing her," but that she is too embarrassed to admit this, even to herself. While using the group sharing technique, she is able to get this insight but does not share any discovery with the group. She simply thanks them for their help and informs them that she was able to understand the dream in the context of her waking life.

CHAPTER 9

THE PROJECTIVE METHOD OF DREAM INTERPRETATION

From Stone Tablets

An actress cannot seem to get her career to take hold. She is constantly looking for work and rarely gets any acting jobs. She dreams that she is in a circle of people, and they are judging her. Suddenly the people burst into flames, and she is in the middle of a ring of fire with no way to escape. The woman decides upon waking to take this dream to her dream group and discuss the imagery with them, hoping to gain insight.

People have been sharing their dreams with one another since the beginning of time. In fact, some of the earliest recordings are from the Mesopotamians who recorded their dreams on stone tablets some five thousand years ago. It seems important and in some cases necessary to share dreams or aspects of the imagery in dreams with others. Simply telling someone else about a dream may help to release feelings associated with it and relieve some of its effects, or it may help bring the imagery into conscious awareness. Whatever the reason, dream sharing has gone on in most cultures for centuries and continues to be a part of the human experience.

The dream group can share and facilitate the actress depending on how they have learned to share dreams. Simply telling the dreamer what they think it means is more damaging than helpful. Sharing dreams is a wonderful and helpful tool but only if it is conducted properly. The Projective Method is one of the most helpful group-sharing techniques, and the actress and her group can use it to help her with her dream imagery and her waking day issues. When using the Projective Method the actress discovers that she is blocked from acting for fear of being "put to the fire."The fact that she may be judged keeps her from fully engaging in the work that she loves.

Safety First

Private, personal, and confidential matters will be embedded in people's dream imagery, so for that reason, dreams should only be shared if the dreamer chooses to do so. When sharing dream material, the dreamer should always feel safe and comfortable with anything that is discussed in the group. Furthermore, the group must agree at the beginning of each session that anything shared in the group stays within the group; issues, imagery, and insights are not to be discussed outside of the session. Once this level of confidentiality is established, group members will feel protected enough to begin working with their dreams. <u>To reiterate this vital point, privacy and confidentially must be upheld and assured to all dreamers who choose to share their dreams and insights with any group</u>.

Projection

Projection is the psychological defense mechanism of attributing one's own characteristics onto others. For example, a woman who is very jealous and envious of other women will constantly assert that other women are jealous and envious of her. This phenomenon can be used to help others see parts of themselves in other people and circumstances. Therefore, when used consciously, this can be a very useful tool. It is this tool that is used in the Projective Method of dream interpretation to help people recognize parts of themselves in situations. When someone has projected a situation, emotion, or thought onto a dreamer's imagery, then the dreamer can tell if this is true by how it feels. If the dreamer "feels" that the person has correctly identified something, then they will have clarity about their imagery.

For example, a woman dreams that she sees a dark shadow of a man lurking in her home. Someone "projects" for her that the man might be someone to be afraid of in waking life. The dreamer recognizes this instantly as her new boss and the fact that she is actually afraid of him. Her emotions tell her that is correct for her.

Do We Need to Know Each Other for This Method?

One of the most valuable facets of the Projective Method is that people who share this method do not have to know each other. In fact, not knowing each other often frees the participants to project openly and honestly, which in the end, may prove even more valuable to the dreamer. The concept of projection is the process of putting one's own thoughts, feelings, and notions onto images or other people, and therefore, knowing each other is not at all necessary.

Projecting with Dreams

A beautiful young woman dreams that she is dating the famous actor Johnny Depp, and they are away together on an idyllic romantic getaway. They are on a beautiful sailboat out in the ocean, and she jumps into the water to swim with the dolphins. The dolphins come to her and dance and swim with her and then safely return her to the sailboat. Johnny Depp is waiting for her with a towel and then wraps the towel around her and lovingly embraces her.

Several authors, writers, and clinicians have shared group techniques of dream interpretation for many years. Though each technique differs in some way or other, the main premise is that by sharing a dream, one is able to gain insight and discovery from others in the group. Discovery will occur when other people who hear the dream provide feedback to the dreamer as if it were their dream.

One such method is the Projective Method of dream interpretation, which has been scientifically tested and shown that the content shared within dreams is directly related to what the dreamer discovers about his or her own life. The method keeps information private and protected for the dreamer and, when used properly, can reveal great insights.

This dreamer gets great insight from each of the members of the group with the Projective Method. The dreamer discovers her deep longing for a loving and connected relationship. After being single for eight years, she is ready for a long-term partner in her life. She also discovers that she longs for a partner that is adventurous, funny, and fun. Her previous partner was very rigid, so she longs for someone who can bring adventure and new experiences to her life.

Projecting in Groups

This method will be discussed in a step-by-step format, which makes it easy to use and easy to teach. Appendix C includes a worksheet for clinicians and group leaders with the instructions so the method can be shared in a formal group setting.

The method can also be used by family members or groups of friends who are interested in dreams and gaining insight from their dreams. The only caution is that the basic rules be followed to ensure that the method is being used to its full advantage.

Basic Rules

1. The group members do not need to know each other.

2. Never, ever, ever tell people what their dream means. The dream is adopted as "your" dream, and you are interpreting it for yourself. The actual dreamer of the dream is simply listening to your version of interpretation.

3. All group members agree not to discuss dreams or images outside of the group unless the dreamer chooses to do so.

Step One: Tools Needed

This method is best used when providing a pen and paper to all participants. This way the group members can write out the dream, and the dreamer can jot down any questions or comments when being provided feedback. Therefore, before starting, everyone should have a pen and paper.

Step Two: Protecting the Group

The second step is to assign one member of the group as the group leader. This person must be familiar with the method and guides the group so the method is conducted in proper order. The group leader first ensures that the important factors of confidentiality, safety, and disclosure in discovery are understood amongst the people in the group. Whenever anyone is willing to share a dream, then his or her dream and its meanings must always be respected by others in the group. This is especially important with the Projective Method because one of the most important issues with this method is that very personal insights may be revealed in the group. This method does *not* require the dreamer to disclose any discovery or meaning, but it may happen due to the nature of the method. For this reason, confidentiality, safety, and discovery must be discussed. The group leader reads out the following passage before the dream is shared:

We are all here to share our projections with each other. Before we begin sharing, we must be reminded of three important principles. First, anything shared in this group will not leave this room. This group is a safe place for us to share with each other, so details of the dream or any projections shared will be kept amongst us. Second, safety is provided here for each of us. We are free to project and share as we agree to keep each other's information safe. Finally, should any personal disclosure occur, we will not discuss it amongst ourselves as that private and personal information is for the dreamer alone.

Step Three: Rules of Disclosure

The third step in the Projective Method is for the group leader to read the following passage directly to the person who will be sharing a dream:

Before you share your dream, we emphasize that no personal disclosure is necessary, and as the dreamer, you can keep all information to yourself throughout the process. Though there is much sharing with this method, you do not have to reveal discovery or insights unless you choose to do so.

Step Four: Sharing and Taking on the Dream

The next step is to allow one of the members of the group to share a dream. In this step, the dreamer shares the dream as it was remembered while group members can make notes if they wish. In this step, group members are taking the dream details on as if it was their dream. For example, if the dreamer says, "I'm standing in my house ..." then group members imagine they are standing in their own house. All members take on the imagery as if it was literally their own imagery and they created it. Instructions are as follows:

One member of the group will now share a dream. Please share the dream in as much detail as possible. Each group member can make notes to remember the dream, but as the dream is being told, we will all adopt the dream *as if it were our own dream imagery.*

The dream then becomes our own dream, and we will speak to it from that point of view.

Step Five: Projecting

When the dream is told in its entirety, then the group leader instructs each participant to project the dream as follows:

We will now each project our interpretation of the dream for the dreamer. We will each, one at a time, reflect back to the dreamer what the dream means for us. Please begin your projection by stating "If this were my dream ..." The dreamer is welcome to make notes or jot down questions for responding to group members after all projections are completed.

Step Six: Back to the Dreamer

When everyone has completed their projection of the dream, then the group leader invites the dreamer to ask members for clarification or more details:

Dreamer, now that everyone has provided a projection, do you have any questions for the members, or is there anything you would like to comment on?

An Example of the Projective Method

Step One: Tools Needed

This method is best used when providing a pen and paper to all participants. This way the group members can write out the dream, and the dreamer can jot down any questions or comments when being provided feedback. Therefore, before starting, everyone should have a pen and paper.

Step Two: Protecting the Group

We are all here to share our projections with each other. Before we begin sharing, we must be reminded of three important principles. First, anything shared in this group will not leave this room. This group is a safe place for us to share with each other, so details of the dream or any projections shared will be kept amongst us. Second, safety is provided here for each of us. We are free to project and share as we agree to keep each other's information safe. Finally, should any personal disclosure occur, we will not discuss it amongst ourselves as that private and personal information is for the dreamer alone.

Step Three: Rules of Disclosure

Before you share your dream, we emphasize that no personal disclosure is necessary, and as the dreamer, you can keep all information to yourself throughout the process. Though there is much sharing with this method, you do not have to reveal discovery or insights unless you choose to do so.

Step Four: Sharing and Taking on the Dream

One member of the group will now share a dream. Please share the dream in as much detail as possible. Each group member can make notes to remember the dream, but as the dream is being told, we will all adopt the dream *as if it were our own dream* imagery. The dream then becomes our own dream, and we will speak to it from that point of view.

Example:

Sixty-year-old male dreamer: I was outside in the front yard. A young male moose with a set of antlers approached and then tried to butt me. He put his head down and tried to butt in a male-dominant role. He persisted and continued, and I tried to fend him off with my hands. I backed away into the house and managed to trap him inside a room where he couldn't get out. I had momentary relief and then looked out the window. I saw my son—he was injured and the buck was running away. My son lamented that the buck had hurt his back. I got angry at my son for being careless and not staying out of the way of the buck when the moose was being wild.

Step Five: Projecting

We will now each project our interpretation of the dream for the dreamer. We will each, one at a time, reflect back to the dreamer what the dream means for us. Please begin your projection by stating "If this were my dream ..." The dreamer is welcome to make notes or jot down questions for responding to group members after all projections are completed.

Group Member 1:

If this were my dream ... it would remind me of my stepfather and my stepbrother. The two of them have constant conflict because my stepbrother constantly gets himself in trouble. My stepfather gets mad at him, and they can't seem to work things out.

Group Member 2:

If this were my dream ... it would be relating to my own anger. The buck/moose reminds me of my inability to control my anger. My anger has hurt many people over the years including my own son. I'm getting better at it now, but I sometimes lash out and can't keep it contained or locked up.

Group Member 3:

If this were my dream ... it would remind me of how much I love camping in the northern wilderness. I have taken my family there for many years, and even though it has been rugged and dangerous at times, it has also been a huge part of our lives together. The adventure has been scary and fun for us as a family, especially my youngest son.

Group Member 4:

If this were my dream ... it would be indicating to me that my son is in danger. Instead of getting angry with him, I should pay attention to what is happening in his life. I am in the house and safe while he is outside and facing some sort of danger. It seems to me that we are separated, and he is in more danger than I. I can control the angry moose but he cannot, and I should be there for him.

Step Six: Back to the Dreamer

Dreamer, now that everyone has provided a projection, do you have any questions for the members, or is there anything you would like to comment on?

Dreamer: I can see that my son and I have had a strained relationship over the years. I have often gotten angry with him while I am always trying to protect him. I can see that I need to look at this relationship more closely and try to not get angry with him in waking day. Thank you for the insights you provided.

CHAPTER 10
DELVING DEEPER INTO THE MEANING OF YOUR DREAMS

The Deepest Level of Being

A man dreams that he is at the doctor's office, and the two of them are looking at an x-ray of his black, tumor-filled lungs. The doctor is showing him the tumors that have developed in each lung. He watches with curiosity and wonders if this is actually happening in his body. Suddenly, his deceased uncle appears before him and begins speaking. Upon waking he can remember the images clearly but cannot remember what his uncle has said to him.

We have learned that thoughts, feelings, waking day behaviors, longings, wishes, and desires are all intimately connected within the dream imagery of each individual; however, people can become disconnected or completely unaware of this phenomenon. For example, thinking about negative events in the past can trigger negative emotions, which in turn, can lead to depressive thoughts, feelings, and behaviors. Dream imagery will then reveal the negative events of the past, the negative emotions of the present, and the negative events of the future if the current pattern is continued. Often this important source of information is often overlooked or ignored. In fact, most often, only the outcome is focused on, such as the depressive behavior in waking day. Rather than seeing the depressed mood as a symptom and using the dream information as a map to guide behavior in a new direction, crucial information is simply overlooked. The dreaming mind fully connects the conscious and unconscious mind and the body. Therefore, it is a direct feedback mechanism on all important matters to the dreamer. Dream imagery will tell you if you're getting sick, if you need to repair your relationship with your kids, if you're in a toxic romantic relationship, if you're blocking your creativity, if you're not practicing self-care; it will report back to you all matters of importance in your life. It is your wisest self speaking directly to you, and it is never wrong.

When the man who dreams of his tumor-filled lungs awakens, he can use meditative dream re-entry to finish his dream. He can follow the procedure and allow the dream to finish unraveling for him. He can also go back to the imagery where his uncle is speaking to him and allow the image of his uncle to come up and tell him what he has forgotten in waking day. The wisdom and crucial information from the dream is not lost when meditative dream re-entry is used.

Meditation and Guided Imagery

Meditation, in all the various forms that it takes, has been a very useful tool for dream interpretation. When the mind is quiet from all mental chatter with meditation, spontaneous insights naturally occur. If dreams are focused on just prior to entering a meditation, insights and discovery will often surface.

Guided imagery is a process where the mind in the meditative state is allowed to focus in a particular direction and then insights and emotions reveal themselves. Both meditation and guided imagery together can be useful for dream interpretation, but several cautions are recommended.

Use with Caution!

It is best not to use meditation and guided imagery when beginning dream interpretation, and therefore, this process is not recommended for novice dream workers.

Many dream interpretation techniques can be used in the early stages of this work. For this reason, the Storytelling Method, the 2A Method, and the Projective Method should be used until discovery and insights become natural. The reason that meditation and guided imagery are not used in the early stages of practice is that these methods may bring up very deep and meaningful insights. In fact, these techniques are designed to do just that. However, if life-altering insights are brought up too quickly into the conscious mind, this may elicit fear or anxiety. As with any practice, whether it be yoga, weight training, or learning a new language, start slowly, master the early steps, and build upon the practice gradually. Once dream interpretation and the insights gained from the practice are comfortable, then the next stage of mastery can occur.

When to Use This Interpretation Method

A man dreams he is walking down a quiet street and notices that he is the only one on the street. Suddenly, a large man jumps out behind him and startles him. He begins to run down a narrow, dark street and feels complete panic and fear. He runs as fast as he can, but he knows this stranger is gaining on him. He wakes up just as the stranger is about to grab his shirt on his back. He has this dream every three to four weeks.

When a dreamer is ready to find deeper meaning and insights into life, then MDR is appropriate. This method is particularly useful for recurring dreams—that is, the same dream imagery that recurs over a long period of time. Generally, recurring dreams carry a message for the dreamer, and once the message is realized and waking day behavior has been changed, the dreams will stop. MDR is useful for fully tapping into the often complex nature of recurring dreams.

MDR is also recommended for dreams with difficult, highly emotional, or confusing imagery. This technique can often untangle difficult dreams where no other technique provides insight. Therefore, anytime a dream is highly confusing, MDR can be used to provide insight. This method is also useful for nightmares; however, if a nightmare is particularly traumatizing, then MDR should only be used in the context of therapy with a trained professional. This method is useful for shifting negative imagery and emotions from dreams but even more useful for traumatic dreams when combined with other forms of therapy. Dream interpretation and especially MDR can be very helpful when used in conjunction with professional guidance.

Finally, MDR is used in dream groups and in group therapy. Since the process of MDR does not require sharing of any kind, groups can use the technique comfortably and safely.

A man does MDR on a recurring dream of being chased down a dark, narrow road by a stranger. When he allows the guided imagery to let the dream unfold, he discovers that this stranger is actually his deceased brother. His brother was always a dark shadow in his life and caused him much distress. MDR suggests that he forgive his brother in waking day and put all negative feelings of the past to rest. Upon waking, he is now able to source out ways to forgive his deceased brother, and as a result, the chasing dreams stop occurring.

The Purpose of MDR

MDR is a technique designed to access the deepest emotional and meaningful connections to the dream imagery and to waking life. At this level of meaning, the entangled emotions, the related events, and the complex problem-solving mechanisms can unfold. Since MDR accesses the deepest levels of being, unconscious material may come up in dreams and provide valuable revelations about one's own life. This is a creative and safe method of letting dreams evolve into the conscious mind. Also, this method has been scientifically tested and was found to lead dreamers to important, life-changing discoveries.

CHAPTER 11
MEDITATIVE DREAM RE-ENTRY

Quiet the Mind

A young woman has a frightening recurring dream that she is drowning and experiencing her own death. She falls off the edge of a dock and feels her heavy body sinking to the bottom of the lake. She can see the sunlight streaming through the water as she is falling, and then suddenly her lungs are piercing with pain as water fills them. She then feels her consciousness leaving her body in a forceful rush of lightness, and she is now dislodged from her own body. She slowly begins to float above the water and watches her own lifeless body continue sinking in the lake.

Meditative Dream Re-entry allows the mind to access the vast and complex landscape of the psyche of which only a portion is actually realized by waking conscious reflection. The underlying emotions, the unconscious desires, and the large storehouse of past memories are all playing and interacting within the landscape, unbeknownst to the individual. It is only when the conscious, rational (and often chatting) mind quiets down that the deeper and complex thoughts and feelings come to the surface of awareness. In order to do this, a peaceful meditation is practiced, and then a visual imagery guides the mind to bring a dream into the quiet mind and allows it continue to evolve.

This form of dream interpretation practice is done by using a guided meditation detailed in this chapter. It is with guided meditation or guided imagery that the dream is allowed to play itself out without conscious obstruction. The result of using this method is that deep thoughts, feelings, and behaviors come alive and reveal the storehouse of knowledge that lies within.

By practicing meditative dream re-entry, the woman drowning in her dreams comes face to face with her own fear of death. Her fear and anxiety surrounding death have led her to making irrational choices in her waking life—moving to cities she does not want to be in, keeping jobs that make her unhappy, and staying in romantic relationships that are anything but romantic for her. By experiencing her own death and making peace with the fact that death is inevitable, she comes to terms with her own time-limited existence and thus begins living each day with awareness and fullness.

What We Know about Meditative Dream Re-Entry (MDR)

Research has found meditative dream re-entry makes several important and unique contributions to the process of discovery and change. One scientific finding is that this dream interpretation technique will significantly lead to discovery about one's life. Interestingly, the discoveries about one's self and life are quite different than discoveries by the other methods. That is, much deeper, richer, and personal information is found with MDR whereas the other methods lead to more concrete and pragmatic information.

For example, a woman had a dream where a stranger appears in the dream, and she is unable to identify the person in waking day. With the Storytelling Method, she is able to identify that this stranger appears in her dreams anytime she is feeling overly stressed in waking day. The 2A Method helps her identify that stress in waking day is accompanied by deep anxiety that is usually experienced when she is facing a new waking day situation. Meditative Dream Re-Entry then helps her access the stranger, who turns out to be her stepfather who was overly critical of her when she was a child. The woman comes to realize that new waking day situations can illicit anxiety and this anxiety brings up the old childhood fear of being criticized. Upon realizing this, she is able to identify the feeling (e.g., "I am feeling afraid here … this is an old familiar feeling") and gently let it go. The feeling no longer controls her life by quietly sneaking up on her without her knowing it. The feeling actually held her back, robbed her of her courage, and kept her stuck when new situations were faced in waking life. MDR allowed her to access this deep and personal part of herself that allowed her to become fully conscious and aware of how she was living her life.

A second significant scientific finding with MDR is that the method can be used for shifting emotions or mood. It has been found that the method is particularly useful for shifting negative or fearful emotions to more positive emotions. If a dreamer wakes feeling sad or distressed from a dream (or a nightmare) then MDR can be used to shift those images and emotions in a positive way.

Studies have also shown that there is a significant difference between groups of people who used MDR for dream interpretation as compared to those who used meditation alone. Meditation is certainly a useful tool for dream interpretation and should be used by those who find this helpful. MDR is another step that adds guided imagery to the process, which has been found to significantly aid in discovery and finding meaning in dreams.

Tools Needed

You will need the following tools in order to do this method. Feel free to draw the dream in your dream journal if you prefer.

1. Guided Meditation described in this chapter
2. Colored crayons for drawing the dream imagery and discovery
3. Instructions from this chapter or from Appendix D
4. Blank paper or a dream journal for recording the dream and drawing

The Procedure of MDR

Before You Begin

Begin relaxation training every day by practicing a short meditation twice a day. It is preferable to practice morning and evening for about ten minutes per session. This meditation should be practiced twice a day for at least fourteen days prior to doing this dream interpretation technique. Unless the mind is able to relax fully with this practice, it is unlikely that MDR can be useful.

Meditation

Sit comfortably with your feet flat on the floor and your hands on your lap with your palms down. Let the chair comfortably hold you so you feel completely safe. Let your body fully relax into the chair so you allow the chair to embrace your body. When you feel very comfortable and can let your body fully sink into the chair, begin the meditation by taking a big breath in. Slowly let the breath fully release and repeat this two more times. After the three big breaths, just sink your weight fully into the chair and let the chair hold you. Let all your muscles relax as much as you can. Let go of any thoughts or tensions you may have. Now sit in this relaxed position for ten minutes. The point of this exercise is to let all thoughts cease for ten minutes. If thoughts come up in the mind, gently imagine they are floating away so they do not take hold.

If it is difficult to sit without racing thoughts for ten minutes then put your awareness onto your breath. Allow the mind to simply watch the breath, without any distractions.

It will take some time to sit for ten minutes without any thoughts as the mind wants to continuously plan, assess, analyze and discuss. This is a practice, so continue to sit by yourself in a comfortable and quiet place, for ten minutes, twice a day. When this relaxation has been mastered, then MDR can be used.

Step 1

1. Write out a dream or one dream scene on a blank paper piece of paper.
2. On the back page of the written dream, draw the dream or some aspect of the dream (e.g., a symbol, a person, a scene) using colored crayons.

Note: You can choose a dream or aspect of a dream that is particularly difficult, confusing, or has negative emotions/imagery. When the drawing has been completed move on to Step 2.

Step 2

Do the relaxation exercise you have been practicing until the mind and body are completely at rest. When you are fully relaxed, do the following visual imagery exercise.

Visual Imagery

When you have practiced the relaxation for at least ten minutes and you are completely relaxed imagine yourself to be sitting in front of a large white screen. Very slowly and very gently, the screen begins to play out the dream or dream scene that you have just drawn. It will appear as a movie for you to watch so slowly allow the dream to play itself out. It may take ten or more minutes, but very slowly and very gently watch the dream that you have drawn come up on the screen.

Once the dream has fully manifested onto the screen and has been playing itself out, then very slowly and very gently allow that dream to become very kind and very loving. Allow love and kindness to slowly let the dream play out and change. Watch the dream play on the screen and note any people, emotions, or images that occur. Let the dream slowly change for you in a loving and peaceful way. Continue watching and make note of any changes that occur.

When the dream is finished playing out in this kind and loving way, it will slowly disappear from the screen. Very slowly and very gently watch the dream dissolve on the screen. When it has fully disappeared, slowly open your eyes and come back to the room.

Step 3

After finishing the relaxation and imagery exercise, go back to your drawing.

Finish the drawing with the crayons as it appeared in your visual imagery.

Draw any changes or shifts that may have occurred during the imagery exercise.

Step 4

Turn the drawing over and write any insights, changes, or discoveries you may have had with this dream interpretation technique with the dream you originally wrote down.

Insights in Sight

It is best to keep the drawings and the discovery passages since insights with MDR tend to unfold over time. You may want to look at it and think about what you discovered, which will allow more information to surface for you. It is suggested that you keep all drawings and dreams in a portfolio or in a dream journal. This will be particularly useful should you need to do MDR again.

It may also be useful to redo MDR if more insight is wanted on a particular dream or image. MDR can be used many times to gain more and more insight into a dream. As dreams provide more information on a subject, MDR can be used to follow through with the dreams. Therefore, MDR and a series of dreams can work together to guide a waking day situation.

For example, a man dreams that he is dating a beautiful woman, but he cannot identify her or where he is upon waking. With MDR he realizes that he is at a local restaurant, and the woman is the owner of that restaurant. He then in waking day visits the restaurant and makes a point of speaking to the owner, whom he now recognizes from his dream. He can now use the dream imagery to guide him in waking day, going to the restaurant and meeting the owner. She may be the woman he would like to date, or she may introduce him to a woman whom he would like to date. Nevertheless, his dreams and MDR can be used as a guide in waking day.

MDR can also be used to shift negative emotions and images in a dream to positive emotions and images. Therefore, any dream imagery that is disturbing, confusing, or fearful can be shifted with MDR in an active way.

A Note to Professionals

Relaxation is generally started on the first day of therapy or group sessions. The process of relaxation is taught, and instructions are given to practice the method twice daily for two weeks (see Appendix D). After one week of relaxation, a discussion about the relaxation process should be undertaken. Any problems encountered should be fully discussed, and suggestions for adjusting the practice may be required.

MDR can be used in session 3 after two weeks of practicing relaxation, if relaxation has been conducted properly. If relaxation is not practiced, it is unlikely that discovery will occur. For severely traumatized patients or for nightmares, additional therapy may be needed prior to using MDR. For major insights gained with MDR, other forms of therapy may be needed for processing these revelations. Professional judgement and sensitivity are required.

During the two week induction period of relaxation, it is suggested that other methods of dream interpretation be used and introduced. Other methods such as the 2A method, the Projective Method, and The Storytelling Method are all appropriate methods for building up toward MDR. These methods will allow the patient to become familiar with the process of discovery, but also, this provides patients tools that can be used in the future along with MDR for continuing the work of self-discovery.

CHAPTER 12
LIVING THE DREAM LIFE

Equipped with the Tools and When to Use Them

The information shared in this book has equipped readers with four scientifically proven dream interpretation techniques. Each of these tools provides a different level of meaning for dreams, and therefore, one dream can be interpreted with all four methods if desired. For very complex and confusing dreams, one method of interpretation may not provide enough meaningful insight, and therefore, it would be wise to use more than one method.

The Storytelling Method is always a good place to start, especially if specific insights about waking day situations are required. For pragmatic situations such as problem solving (How can I decrease my stress at work?), emotional regulation (How can I feel better in my difficult marriage?), or guidance on specific matters (When will I feel most spiritually fulfilled?), TSM will provide direct information (e.g. You are taking on too much work, which is causing stress). This method is best used when an answer to a specific situation or question is being sought. For more emotionally charged information, the 2A Method can access that best.

The 2A Method helps to tease out the emotions that are often buried or entangled within other forms of information. This method can help with relationship issues (Why do I feel so lonely?), health-related information (What emotion is feeding into my heart disease?), family matters (How can I best help my drug-addicted daughter?), and general emotional states (Why am I depressed?). Of course, we are often not aware of what solutions we really need, so using more than one method will provide more insight and better direction. The Storytelling Method might indicate that the stress in one's life is being caused by taking on too much at work, and then the 2A Method reveals that anxiety is the underlying reason for taking the work on. The 2A Method may show that the feelings of anxiety are being fed by the work stress and that this has set up a vicious cycle. By realizing both of these important pieces to the puzzle (anxiety leads to taking on more work, which leads to more anxiety), the dreamer can begin making changes in waking day. However, sharing one's dreams with other people adds yet another valuable system to obtaining insights.

When a dream is particularly confusing or the dreamer would simply like to share it, then the Projective Method is a very good choice for interpretation. This method is always helpful, and often the simple act of sharing opens the doors for more dream work to happen. The Projective Method may provide the insight directly, or some aspect of the insight, so another method can be used until the full meaning is obtained. No matter how much or how little is revealed, this method is extremely valuable in formal dream groups, with family members, or with other dream enthusiasts.

Finally, MDR provides the deepest, innermost meaning to dreams. This method can be used for all dreams at all times, and it never disappoints. Of course this method should be used once readers are accustomed to doing all three dream interpretations of TSM, the 2A Method, and the Projective Method. This way dream insights and meaning will be a natural course of the day.

Becoming Conscious

Beginning and committing to a dream interpretation practice is one of the best gifts anyone can give to themselves. The information received from dreams and interpretations will be invaluable to one's life. This is truly the greatest guidance anyone could ever ask for. Most importantly, the information will help all dreamers become more conscious in their lives, both in their waking and dreaming lives. A conscious life is one that is richer, happier, and purpose driven. If dream interpretation is also combined with a regular meditation practice, daily prayer, inspirational readings, chanting, therapy, yoga, or any other self-development practice, then consciousness in dream life and waking life will provide constant, invaluable, life-enhancing information.

Living the Dream

Realizing one's own stream of consciousness and then participating in its evolution will change the direction of life forever, and always for the better. It is only by becoming conscious and then participating with the masterful, pervasive intelligence that directs all life that one's life will be lived to the fullest. By following one's own dreams, information between the challenges in the physical world and the direction transmitted in dreams can transform life to the way it is meant to be.

CHAPTER 13
THE TRANSFORMATIVE POTENTIAL OF DREAMS

Let the Transformation Begin

Why can't I find my soul mate? Why is my job not reward-ing? Why can't we get pregnant? Should I take my savings and travel to Europe? Is this cancer treatment working for me? How can I feel better about myself? Am I addicted to alcohol? How do I recover from this divorce? The answer to all these questions and more, which lie at the heart of good health and happiness, are simply within each and every individual. Every person is the expert on his or her own life and its path, but the key is to first find the answers deep within the self, then bring them into conscious awareness, and finally, adjust wak-ing life accordingly. Therefore, the three important steps are (1) to find the answers by recording all dreams, (2) become consciously aware of the answers by doing dream interpre-tation, and (3) adjust waking life accordingly. If dreams have recurring imagery of a scary, violent man and interpretations repeatedly reveal that it is time to get out of a current rela-tionship because it is toxic, then waking day behaviors have to be adjusted to that awareness. In waking day, the dreamer will get finances in order, start making new living arrange-ments, and begin the recovery process from that relationship. Only by doing all three steps and following through in waking day can life transform to its greatest creation.

We know that the dreaming mind taps into the most com-plex level of being: the conscious and unconscious thoughts, feelings, behaviors, experiences, longings, and desires that are entangled together. Dreams are the source of informa-tion that exists between the physical world and the nonphysi-cal, so only by listening and then following through on this guidance will life change. This is the place where everyone can find their unique life path to health and happiness; this is literally the life of your dreams.

Making It Work

When committing to living a more conscious life through dream work, one must realize that dream life and waking life are one and the same. The mind does not shut itself off upon sleeping, and in fact, it just keeps processing from waking state to dream state back to waking state. During the dream state, the mind is the same mind as it was while awake, but more information is being processed. Consciousness is a continuous process while awake and while asleep and paying attention to both phases is what makes a fully conscious and purposeful life. Therefore, paying attention to dreams, doing interpretation, and then making adjustments in waking life is the full cycle that transforms life to its highest purpose.

Wake up and Smell the Coffee: Attend

A woman dreams that she is on an elevator and when the doors open, she meets a brick wall and can't get off. She feels unusually calm and unafraid. She notices that she is holding a cup of hot coffee and watches the steam rising from the cup.

Do not ignore dream imagery! When people have a dream that they don't like, they tend to ignore it with the old adage: "It's just a dream." We now know that this should be replaced with "It's a dream: attend, interpret, act." A dream comes up anytime there is something important to be made aware of, and the intelligence in the dreaming mind is alerting the dreamer to this. This information is the most valuable source of information anyone could ever receive. Make it your mantra for dreams: attend, interpret, act.

The woman who finds herself in the elevator with a cup of coffee and a brick wall discovers in dream interpretation that she must "wake up and smell the coffee." For her, this means to stop waiting for people to come along and save her, to stop waiting for a better day, and to literally start making a life for herself. She can now become aware of her old bad habits in waking day that are contributing to her stagnation or hitting a brick wall. Her awareness plus commitment to change will lead her to a whole new life.

Dreams Are Your Best Friend: Interpret

One of the major blocks to working with dreams is the fact that people are afraid of the information they may receive. What if a dream foreshadows death or illness? What if dream interpretation reveals that a relationship should end? What if it reveals an addiction or health-compromising behavior? The most important fact to remember with dreams is that they will always provide information that will benefit the dreamer. If an illness is impending, then the dream will be a warning so medical attention can be sought. If a relationship is toxic, then the dreams will reveal a path to a more nourishing and loving relationship. This may mean ending the current relationship in order to receive a better one. Dreams will not abandon the dreamer (often people give up before the information has revealed itself) nor will they lead the dreamer in the wrong direction. The dreaming mind is a part of the evolution of the human species, so dreams occur for a reason. Dreams occur to help and guide the dreamer.

Seeing the Landmarks: Act

Dream insights and imagery must be matched to waking life experiences in order to be truly useful. By allowing the insights to guide waking behavior, one's life will begin to transform. For example, the woman who dreams of having coffee in an elevator with a brick wall discovers that she needs to make changes in her life before her life will improve. Upon reflection, she becomes aware of the fact that she has become very lazy, very tired, and overweight. She will always take the elevator rather than the stairs, even if it's just one floor. She has reduced her mobility as much as possible. A few days after her dream and insight she sees a sign that reads: "Walk for your health." After remembering her insight, she decides to make a new choice by walking whenever she can, including walking stairs instead of taking the elevator. By slowly adopting these choices, her energy will increase, her weight will decrease, and she will begin feeling better. She can then continue working with her dreams to improve other matters in her life such as her eating patterns, her job, and her emotions. By working with the dreams and acting on the guidance, she is becoming a cocreator with her higher self.

Pointing in the Right Direction

Once dream work has been incorporated into one's life, then waking day circumstances and life conditions will be in perfect synch with dreams. A woman was away on a business trip and felt nervous that she might be late for her very important meeting the next day. She dreams that she is in a meeting and sees a clock with the time 7:00 a.m. Upon waking and going to find her meeting, she decides to leave at 7:00 a.m. though this appears very early to her. As a result, the traffic is very bad in that city, and she just makes it to her meeting on time. By paying attention to the dream information in waking day, she discovers that her concern of being late was completely justified. The conscious awareness of the information from the dream is that which directs life. Therefore, this information should be considered in all aspects of life and especially when making decisions. As a dreamer gets more and more comfortable with the practice of dream interpretation, there will be a direct line of communication between the physical world conditions of the dreamer and the nonphysical world of dream imagery. This information can be used when changing jobs, choosing careers, choosing life partners, finding a home, increasing abundance, parenting and coparenting, traveling, learning new skills, caregiving to elderly parents—the guidance is absolutely endless.

One last and very important note about taking action in waking life from dream guidance is that *happiness can never come from causing pain to others.* This must be considered before taking any waking day action. For example, taking up a relationship with a married man or causing another person to lose his or her job is not the highest path to one's own happiness. Action in waking life must be undertaken with responsible, ethical choice at all times.

Clear Sailing

The most powerful purpose of dreams is to help the dreamer find his or her true life passions and purpose. Dreams will help sort through difficult emotions and inner conflicts and ultimately lead the dreamer in the direction for living the most fulfilling life. There is a calling and a purpose in each and every person, but often that calling gets confused with difficult life challenges (I don't have enough money to do it), with conflicting information (If I do it I may be unhappy), with confusing guidance (My parents will hate it if I do it); the distractions from purpose and happiness are endless. The information from dreams takes the highest form of guidance from the nonphysical intelligence and presents itself in dreams for application in physical world circumstances. This intelligence is the greatest guide, the most accurate navigator, and the greatest source of love anyone could ever hope for. *Sweet dreams.*

Appendix A

The Storytelling Method of Dream Interpretation

Step 1

Write your dream in the space below. Write in full sentences and with as much detail as possible. For long dreams, write each dream scene on a separate worksheet.

Step 2

Go back to the dream on the previous page and underline the most important or "salient" word or phrase for you in each sentence.

Step 3(a) Write the underlined words in the order that they appear in the dream in Section A below.

Section A	Section B

Step 3(b) Go back to the table on the previous page and put down in Section B the first word that comes to mind for you for each word in Section A.

Step 4

Take the words in Section B and write a short and simple story with the words. Keep the words <u>in the order that they appear</u> in the list. The story should make sense to you.

Step 5

Answer the following questions:

a) Does this story have meaning for you? Explain.

b) Does this story relate to your waking life in some way? Explain.

c) Does this story relate to any <u>specific events</u> in your waking life?

d) Did this analysis give you any clear insight? _____ yes _____ no

e) If yes, write about the insight and how it relates to your life.

APPENDIX B
THE 2A METHOD OF DREAM INTERPRETATION

Step 1: Write Out Your Dream

In the space below, write your dream as you remember it. Include as much detail as possible. If you have several dream scenes, then record each scene on a separate worksheet and interpret each scene separately.

Step 2: Key Words and Phrases

Go back to your dream on the previous page and circle or underline up to ten or fifteen key words or phrases that stand out for you. If you have more than 10–15 words, you can put those on another worksheet. Keep the words in the order that they appear.

Step 2(a): Words and Associations

Take the words that you circled or underlined and write them in Column A below. Keep the words in the order that they appear in the dream.

Column A   Column B

Step 2(b)

Write in Column B, on the previous page, the first word that comes to mind for each word that is written in column A. Keep the words in the order that they appear.

Step 3: Amplification

1) Write the words from Column B in the order they appear in Section 1 on the next page.

2) Fill in Section 2 by answering the questions below.

> **What does this word remind you of?**
>
> **How is this word related to you in your life?**
>
> **Who reminds you of this word in your waking life?**
>
> **Where are you in relation to this word?**
>
> **Why does this word relate to you in some way?**

3) Write three emotions in Section 3 that the words in Section 2 remind you of.

Step 3: Table

Section 1: Words From Column B	Section 2: Questions to Answer For Each Word	Section 3: 3 Emotions
	What does this word remind you of?	
	How is this word related to you in your life??	
	Who reminds you of this word in your waking life?	
	Where are you in relation to this word?	
	Why does this word relate to you in some way?	

Step 4: Insight

Read over the words from Section 2 and the feelings in Section 3 that are associated with your words. Read this over several times and then answer the following questions:

Do these words and feelings make any sense to you?

Does this relate to you personally in any way?

Do the words and feelings relate to any specific events in your waking life?

Do the words and feelings remind you of anyone else's life situation?

Appendix C
The Projective Method of Dream Interpretation

Step One: Tools Needed

This method is best used when providing a pen and paper to all participants. This way the group members can write out the dream, and the dreamer can jot down any questions or comments when being provided feedback. Therefore, before starting, everyone should have a pen and paper.

Step Two: Protecting the Group

We are all here to share our projections with each other. Before we begin sharing, we must be reminded of three important principles. First, anything shared in this group will not leave this room. This group is a safe place for us to share with each other, so details of the dream or any projections shared will be kept amongst us. Second, safety is provided here for each of us. We are free to project and share as we agree to keep each other's information safe. Finally, should any personal disclosure occur, we will not discuss it amongst ourselves as that private and personal information is for the dreamer alone.

Step Three: Rules of Disclosure

Before you share your dream, we emphasize that no personal disclosure is necessary, and as the dreamer, you can keep all information to yourself throughout the process. Though there is much shar-

ing with this method, you do not have to reveal discovery or insights unless you choose to do so.

Step Four: Sharing and Taking on the Dream

One member of the group will now share a dream.
Please share the dream in as much detail as possible.
Each group member can make notes to remember
the dream, but as the dream is being told, we will all
adopt the dream *as if it were our own dream imagery*.
The dream then becomes our own dream, and we
will speak to it from that point of view.

Step Five: Projecting

We will now each project our interpretation of
the dream for the dreamer. We will each, one at a
time, reflect back to the dreamer what the dream
means for us. Please begin your projection by stating
"If this were my dream ..." The dreamer is welcome
to make notes or jot down questions for responding to group members after all projections are
completed.

Step Six: Back to the Dreamer

Dreamer, now that everyone has provided a projection, do you have any questions for the members,
or is there anything you would like to comment on?

APPENDIX D
MEDITATIVE DREAM RE-ENTRY

Before You Begin

Begin relaxation training every day by practicing a short medita-
tion twice a day. It is preferable to practice morning and eve-
ning for about ten minutes per session. This meditation should be
practiced twice a day for at least fourteen days prior to doing this
dream interpretation technique. Unless the mind is able to relax
fully with this practice, it is unlikely that MDR can be useful.

Meditation

Sit comfortable with your feet flat on the floor and your
hands on your lap with palms facing down. Let the chair
comfortably hold you so you feel completely safe. Let your
body fully relax into the chair so you allow the chair to
embrace your body. When you feel very comfortable and
can let your body fully sink into the chair, begin the meditation by taking a big breath in. Slowly let the breath fully
release and repeat this two more times. After the three big
breaths, just sink your weight fully into the chair and let the
chair hold you. Let all your muscles relax as much as you can.
Let go of any thoughts or tensions you may have. Now sit in
this relaxed position for ten minutes. The point of this exercise is to let all thoughts cease for ten minutes. If thoughts
come up in the mind, gently imagine they are floating away
so they do not take hold.

If it is difficult to sit without racing thoughts for ten minutes then put your awareness onto your breath. Allow the
mind to simply watch the breath, without any distractions.

It will take some time to sit for ten minutes without any
thoughts as the mind wants to continuously plan, assess, ana-

lyze and discuss. This is a practice, so continue to sit by yourself in a comfortable and quiet place, for ten minutes, twice a day. When this relaxation has been mastered, then MDR can be used.

Step 1

1. Write out the dream or one dream scene on a blank piece of paper.

2. On the back page of the written dream, draw the dream or some aspect of the dream (e.g., a symbol, a person, a scene) using colored crayons.

Note: You can choose a dream or an aspect of a dream that is particularly difficult, confusing or has negative emotions/imagery. When you have completed the drawing, move on to Step 2.

Step 2

Do the meditation exercise that has been practiced for the past two weeks. When fully relaxed, bring up a visual imagery of "the dream scene" that is in the drawing. Continue to visualize the dream and let it play out completely.

Once the dream has been fully imagined, begin slowly infusing the dream with love and peacefulness. Allow the dream to play out completely with love. Do this step slowly and calmly until the dream has played itself out to the end.

Step 3

After finishing the relaxation and imagery exercises go back to your drawing. Finish the drawing with the crayons as it appeared in your visual imagery. Draw any changes or shifts that may have occurred during the imagery exercise.

Step 4

Turn the drawing over and write any insights, changes, or discoveries you may have had with this dream interpretation technique with the dream you originally wrote down.

APPENDIX E
RECOMMENDED READINGS

This section outlines some of the research that was mentioned throughout the book. Research on dreams and the consciousness of dreaming is very vast and often very complicated. The articles and books in this section are a selection of readings and are intended for readers who want to consult the literature. This is in no way an exhaustive list as the study and writings of dreams and dreaming has been built upon since the beginning of time.

Beck, A. T. 1971. *Dream dynamics: Science and psychoanalysis.* New York: Grune & Stratton.

Bonime, W. 1962. *The clinical use of dreams.* New York: Basic Books.

Boss, M., and B. Kenny, eds. 1987. *Dream interpretation: A comparative study,* 149–189.

Cartwright, R., M. Agargun, J. Kirkby, and J. Friedman. 2006. Relations of dreams to waking concerns. *Psychiatry Research* 141:261-270.

DeCicco, T. L. 2008. Pondering the consequences of uninterpreted dreams. *Dreamtime.* Winter, 12–13.

DeCicco, T. L. 2007. What is the story telling? Examining discovery with The Storytelling Method (TSM) and testing with a control group. *Dreaming* 17:227–237.

DeCicco, T. L. 2007. Dreams of female university students: Content analysis and relationship to discovery via the Ullman method. *Dreaming* 17 (2): 98–112.

DeCicco, T., D. King, and T. Humphreys. 2007. What sex dreams really mean: Examining discovery of dreams with sexual content. *In press.*

DeCicco, T.L., G. Navara, D.B. King, C. Moran, H. Higgins, and A. Smit, 2008. Dreaming about major life issues: Pain, relationships, addictions & breast cancer. Papers presented at the *25th Annual Conference of the International Association for the Study of Dreams*, Montreal, Que.

DeCicco, T. L. and D.B. King. 2008. Meditative Dream Re-Entry: Discovery and Emotional Shifting with Dreams. Workshop presented at to the *25th Annual Conference of the International Association for the Study of Dreams*, Montreal, Que.

Domhoff, G.W. 1996. *Finding meaning in dreams: A quantitative review.* New York: Plenum Press.

Domhoff, G. W. 2000. *Moving dream theory beyond Freud and Jung.* Paper presented to the symposium "Beyond Freud and Jung?" Berkeley, CA.

Gilchrist, S., J. Davidson, and J. Shakespeare-Finch. 2007. Dream emotions, waking emotions, personality characteristics and well-being—A positive approach. *Dreaming* 17 (3): 172–185.

Goelitz, A. 2001. Nurturing life with dreams: Therapeutic dream work with cancer patients. *Clinical Social Work Journal* 29 (4): 375–388.

Hill, C. E. 2003. *Working with dreams: Facilitating exploration, insight, and action.* Washington, DC: American Psychological Association.

Hill, C. E., J. S. Zack, T. L. Wonnell, M. Hoffman, A. B. Rochlen, J. L. Goldberg, E. Y. Nakayama, K. J. Heaton, F. A. Kelley, K. Eiche, M. J. Tomlinson, and S. Hess. 2000. Structured brief therapy with a focus on dreams or loss for clients with troubling dreams and recent loss. *Journal of Counseling Psychology* 47 (1): 90–101.

King, D. B., and T. L. DeCicco. 2007. The relationship among dream content, physical health, mood and self-construal. *Dreaming* 17 (3): 127–139.

Krippner, S., and J. Weinhold. 2002. Gender differences in a content analysis study of 608 dream reports from research participants in the United States. *Social Behavior and Personality* 30 :399–410.

Mellman, T.A., D. David, V. Bustamante, J. Torres, and A. Fins. 2001. Dreams in the acute aftermath of trauma and their relationship to PTSD. *International Society for Traumatic Stress Studies* 14 (1): 241–253.

Ohaeri, J.U., O.B. Campbell, A. O. Ilesanmil, and B.M. Ohaeri. 1998. Psychosocial concerns of Nigerian women with breast and cervical cancer. *Psycho-Oncology* 7 (6): 494–501.

Pessant, N., and A. Zadra. 2004. Working with dreams in therapy: What do we know and what should we do? *Clinical Psychology Review* 24:489–512.

Picchioni, D., B. Goeltzenleucher, D. N. Green, M. J. Convento, R. Crittenden, M. Hallgren, and R. A. Hicks. 2002. Nightmares as a coping mechanism for stress. *Dreaming* 12 (3): 155–173.

Punamaki, R. 1998. The role of dreams in protecting psychological well-being in traumatic conditions. *International Journal of Behavioral Development* 22 (3): 559–588.

Punamaki, R., K. J. Ali, K. H. Ismahil, and J. Nuutinen, J. 2005. Trauma, dreaming, and psychological distress among Kurdish children. *Dreaming* 15 (3): 178–194.

Schredl, M. 2001. Dreams of singles: effects of waking-life social contacts on dream content. *Personality and Individual Differences* 31:269–275.

Schredl, Ciric, Bishop, Goliz, and Buschtons. Content analysis of German students' dreams: Comparison to American findings. *Dreaming* 13.

Schredl, M. and F. Hoffman. 2003. Continuity between waking activities and dream activities. *Consciousness and Cognition* 12:298–308.

Schredl, M., V. Sahin, and G. Schafer. 1998. Gender differences in dreams: do they reflect gender differences in waking life? *Personality and Individual Differences* 25:433–442.

Ullman, M. 1996. *Appreciating dreams: A group approach.* Thousand Oaks, CA: Sage Publications.

Ullman, M., and N. Zimmerman. 1979. *Working With Dreams.* New York: Dellacorte Press.

Van de Castle, R. L. 1969. Some problems in applying the methodology of content analysis to dreams. In *Dream Psychology and the New Biology of Dreaming,* ed. M. Kramer. Springfield, IL: Charles Thomas.

Van de Castle, R. L. 1994. *Our dreaming mind.* New York: Random House, Inc.

Ward, C. H., A. T. Beck, and E. Rascoe. 1961. Typical dreams. Incidence among psychiatric patients. *Archives of General Psychiatry* 5:606-615.

Zadra, A. 2007. Sex dreams: What do men and women dream about? *Sleep* 30:A376.

Zadra, A., and C. C. Donderi. 2000. Prevalence of nightmares and bad dreams and their relationship to psychological well-being. *Journal of Abnormal Psychology* 109:210–219.

CPSIA information can be obtained at www.ICGtesting.com
Printed in the USA
LVOW121623100912

298201LV00002B/3/P